The two greatest
commandments.

The word is for everyone.
The word of God is for everyone!

The Life and Teachings of Jesus

Douglas A. Leas

Griz Press, LLC.

ISBN 978-1-937297-07-7
Library of Congress Control Number: 2024901318
Published in the United States of America
First printing, January 2024.

Griz Press, LLC.
Jacksonville, FL.
www.GrizPress.com

Cover design by Douglas A. Leas

The cover images are famous depictions of Jesus from various time periods:

Top left: Jesus Christ Deësis mosaic by n.d., c. 1261, Hagia Sophia.

Top right: Divine Mercy by Kazimirowski Eugeniusz, 1934.

Middle left: Christ Carrying the Cross by Titian, 1508.

Middle right: The Last Supper by Willem Jacob Herreyns, c. 1790-1800.

Bottom left: Christ and the Rich Young Ruler by Heinrich Hofmann, 1889.

Bottom right: Christ with beard by n.d., c. 4th century, Catacomb of Commodilla,

All images are Public Doman from Wikimedia Commons.

See www.GrizPress.com for other books and short stories by Douglas A. Leas.

This book is dedicated to Jesus, who inspired
billions with his teachings.

Special thanks to Corrine and Jeff
for putting up with me through
this journey and for their valuable
perspectives and feedback.

Contents

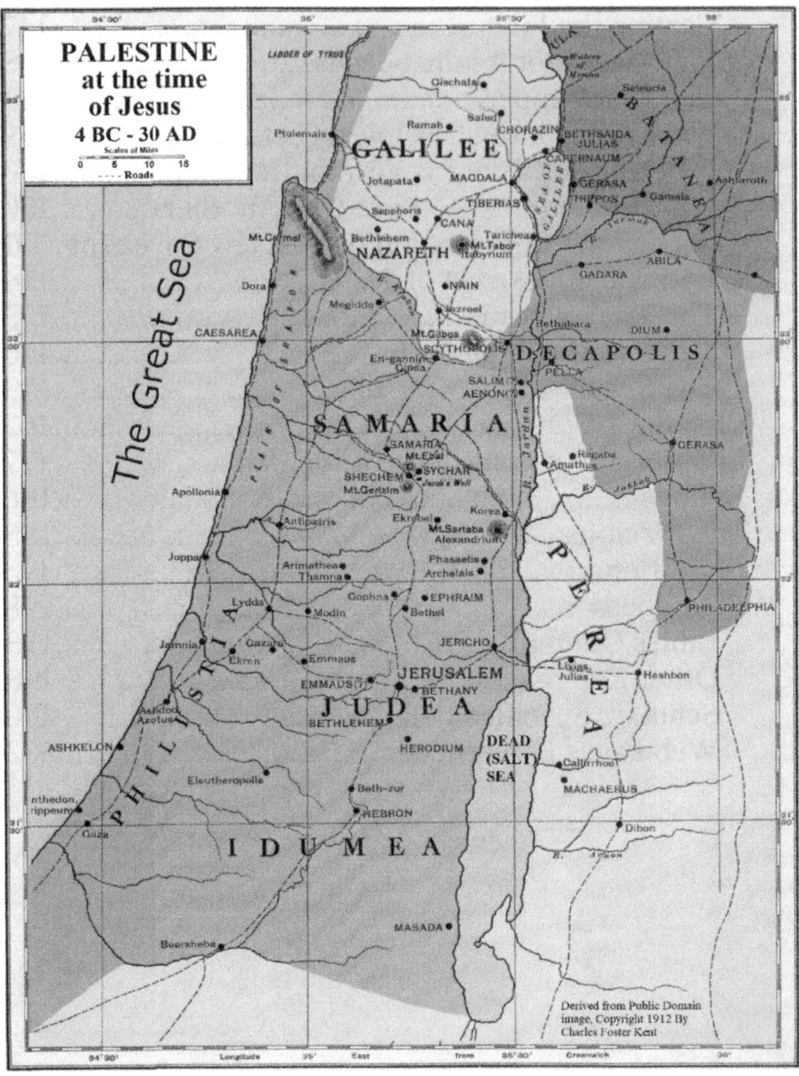

During Jesus' early life, Herod the Great's sons ruled most of his prior kingdom. Herod Archelaus ruled Samaria, Judea, and Idumea. Herod Antipas ruled Galilee and Perea. Phillip ruled Batanea, Trachonitis, and Gaulanitis. The Decapolis area contained free city-states under Roman protection. Archelaus was replaced by a series of Roman governors (prefects) starting in 6 AD. Pontius Pilate was the prefect during Jesus' ministry.

Introduction

You may be thinking, "Yet another book about Jesus! Why write another book on this topic? What does this book have to offer that others may not?" This work started as a personal investigation of Jesus' teachings unfettered by any specific church's views. I was raised in a Christian family and attended a Protestant (Methodist) church in my youth. As many do, when I was a teen and young adult, I had questions, and I did not find adequate answers from my parents or church, and I drifted away, unsure of what I believed. Over the years, I sought answers to my questions from people of various faiths and denominations, but I was not convinced these answers were correct.

I finally decided it was time to figure out what Jesus taught, not what various other people, churches, or denominations say he taught, so I could decide what I believe. It has been quite a journey, and I discovered that many things I had been taught or told do not reflect Jesus' teachings accurately. As I made various discoveries or had personal revelations and discussed them with others, the idea of writing this all down came up. Some people were eager to read it and encouraged me to get it down on paper and share it with others. So, I decided to undertake that project.

I have done my best to examine the sources, read the analysis of learned scholars, and understand the views of the Catholic Church, various Protestant Denominations, and non-believers as they relate to Jesus' life and teachings. I also endeavored to understand the historical context and to figure out what Jesus taught as best I could around 1,990 years after the fact. (Jesus is thought to have started his ministry between 27 and 29 AD and died between 30 and 33 AD.)

I decided to try to make this a book that would appeal to the average person who wants a summary of who Jesus was, his life, and what he taught. I tried to avoid making it a dry academic exercise that would be of interest to few or a preachy diatribe. You, the reader, can decide if I have accomplished that goal.

Unless expressly stated otherwise, the information discussed in this book is not my opinion. I attempted to figure out what Jesus taught, then explain, and summarize it as best I could. Some of it will be controversial because people do not like some of what Jesus taught. It would be immoral to misrepresent Jesus' teachings to suit current societal norms, so I have endeavored to represent them correctly.

The primary sources for information about the life and teachings of Jesus are the Gospels of Matthew, Mark, Luke, and John and The Acts of the Apostles, contained in the New Testament. However, other books of the New Testament and historical sources outside the

Bible were consulted as well. I have included a chapter in the book that discusses my sources and the current thinking and controversies about their origins and a chapter about the versions or translations of the Bible used. If you prefer to read about those sources before reading about the life and teachings of Jesus, please jump to those chapters first.

How to read this book

This book is intended to summarize who Jesus was, his life, and what he taught. Some people want more of a summary than others, and others may be interested in specific teachings of Jesus. To help the reader, I have supplied a table of contents and made each topic its own section so you can easily find what you are looking for. In longer sections, I have provided a summary and a more detailed discussion. That way, you can read the level of detail that interests you. I also provide a list of definitions of uncommon words and a brief list of resources and references at the end of the book for those who want to read more.

The Bible quotes in this book come from The *New American Bible Revised Edition NABRE* or The *English Standard Version ESV*. I marked each quote showing which translation I quoted with (NABRE) or (ESV). In each case, I picked a translation that agreed with most translations and avoided minority translations. When substantive differences exist between these two, I quote one and show the difference in braces [like this]. See the Versions of the Bible chapter for more details.

Chapter 1: The Life of Jesus

This section describes what the Bible says about the life of Jesus and what some other sources say about his life. It also addresses the significant controversies or differing points of view related to his life. Let us start at the beginning with Jesus' birth.

The Birth of Jesus

This section covers when and where Jesus was born, according to the Gospels.

Summary

- Jesus existed; he is not made up.
- Jesus was born in Bethlehem in Judea, which is in the West Bank today.
- Jesus was either born in a stable or in a cave or grotto used as an animal shelter and for storage, possibly on Joseph's family's property.
- His mother was named Mary and was later referred to as Mary of Nazareth.
- His father was either God via virgin birth or an unknown person. Joseph of Nazareth is recorded as his adoptive father in the Bible.

- Jesus was born between 6 BC and 2 BC
- We do not know what month and day Jesus was born. Most Christians celebrate his birth on December 25th.
- Jesus is thought to be descended from King David and Abraham of the Old Testament.

Discussion

We know from the Gospels of Matthew and Luke that Jesus was born in Bethlehem in Judea in what is today the West Bank. It is located just south of Jerusalem. His mother was Mary of Nazareth. Nazareth is a town in Israel about midway between the Mediterranean Sea and the Sea of Galilee, sixty-four miles north of Jerusalem. There seems to be disagreement between the gospels of Luke and Matthew as to whether Mary was just engaged to Joseph of Nazareth or if they were married at the time of the birth of Jesus.

Matthew 1:18 refers to Joseph and Mary as betrothed but not living together when Mary was found to be with child. Matthew 1:19 describes Joseph as Mary's husband and that he planned to divorce her quietly after discovering that she was pregnant. However, Matthew 1:20-25 describes an angel visiting Joseph in a dream, telling him that she was a virgin and that the Holy Spirit performed a miracle and caused Mary to conceive a child. So, Joseph takes Mary into his home but has no relations with her until after Jesus is born.

Luke 2:1 describes Mary and Joseph as betrothed at the time of the birth of Jesus. At that time, Jewish law held that a couple was not married until they consummated their marriage, so they may have had a marriage ceremony before Jesus was born but did not consummate the marriage until after. If that were the case, it would fit both accounts.

In either case, these gospels make it clear that Joseph was Jesus' adoptive father, not his biological father. Non-believers and early opponents of Christianity think that either Joseph was Jesus' father or that Mary had an affair. One theory, circulated by Celsus (a Greek philosopher in the second century), holds that Mary had an affair with a Roman soldier named Pantera, but there is no objective evidence of that, and as Will Durant concluded in his well-known history, *"Caesar and Jesus"* these statements appear to be *"clumsy fabrications."* This story was likely concocted to discredit Jesus.

Much is written about the possibility that the virgin birth part of the story was made up later to align the story with prophecy. The Gospels of Matthew and Luke both contain the story of the virgin birth of Jesus, and they were written in the first century. This idea was widely accepted by the Christian church in the second century. It is impossible to know the truth at this point over two thousand years later. Early Christians believed it, but the truth of the virgin birth is a matter of faith.

According to Luke 2:1, Joseph and Mary were in Bethlehem because Caesar Augustus ordered a census when Quirinius was governor of Syria, which required families to go back to where they were from (apparently the husband's place of origin not the wife's). Luke's account says Joseph traveled to Bethlehem to be registered with Mary. It does not say that Mary had to travel, as the popular recounting of the story indicates. This implies that Mary may have already been there. Because of the census, Bethlehem was crowded, and the inn was full, so Jesus was born in a place where animals were kept, and he was laid in a manger (an animal feeding trough). While people assume he was born in a barn, the Bible does not describe the place; it just mentions the manger. There are many papers and books that discuss this account.

Joseph was from Bethlehem, and his family had property there. The word translated as "*inn*" can also mean "*guest room*" or "*large room*" and may have referred to a part of the family property. Some scholars suggest that Luke is saying that the house was full, and privacy was needed for birth, so it is theorized that they moved Mary to a cave, used for storage and keeping prized animals on the property to give birth. Many homes in that area were built by or over caves used for various purposes. The place marked as the birthplace of Jesus in Bethlehem today is such a cave.

Justin Martyr (100-165 AD), a Greek philosopher and early supporter of Christianity, wrote that Jesus was born in a cave outside the village of Bethlehem. Early theologians like Origen of Alexandria (185-254 AD) mention the rumor that Jesus was born in a cave and said that pilgrims in his time, about 248 AD, visited such a cave. In 313 AD, Emperor Constantine declared Christianity acceptable in the Edict of Milan. Later, in about 326 AD, he sent his mother Helena to identify sites from Jesus' life, and she identified the site of the current

Grotto of the Nativity in Bethlehem as Jesus' birthplace. I tried to determine if the early or any present church took an official position on this question. Both in ancient writings and current articles, there are references to the tradition that Jesus was born in a cave, and they refer to the same sources I mentioned above. As far as I can tell, they do not take an official position on this topic, but they admit it is possible.

Interestingly, Matthew does not mention a census, a journey late in Mary's pregnancy, or the inn being full and simply states that Jesus was born in Bethlehem of Judea. Some scholars think that Luke incorrectly believed that Joseph and Mary lived in Nazareth and was trying to explain why they had to journey to Bethlehem and that the census part of the story is simply incorrect. Reading just Matthew, you might conclude that Joseph and Mary lived in Bethlehem and moved to Nazareth later.

The gospels go on to describe related events like a bright star in the sky, angels appearing to the shepherds tending their flocks, a visit from the wise men, and Herod the Great (the local Roman client king) learning that a child foretold by prophecy as the King of the Jews was born in Bethlehem. The Bible mentions that Herod later ordered the killing of all the male children under two years old born in Bethlehem in an attempt to kill the child foretold by prophecy.

Some of these details have been used to attempt to determine the year that Jesus was born. Multiple passages in the Bible refer to him being born during the reign of Herod. The Jewish historian Flavius Josephus (c. 94 AD) recorded details of Herod's death occurring after a day that the Jews observe as a fast which happened just before an eclipse of the moon and before the Passover (Jewish Antiquities XVII, Ch 13).

He also mentioned several other events that occurred at the time. These writings were used to produce a date for Herod's death in about 4 BC that was widely accepted for a time. However, more recent scholars have uncovered evidence that could place Herod's death as late as 1 BC. For example, physics professor John A. Cramer, in a letter to the Biblical Archaeology Society (BAR) in 2013, points out that that there were four lunar eclipses visible in that area and time frame, one in 5 BC (total eclipse), one in 4 BC (partial eclipse), and two in 1 BC (one total and one partial). Based on the dates of the eclipses and potential fasts and Passover bracketing the events, he suggests that one of the eclipses in 1 BC works better than the one in 4 BC to match that information. Gerard Gertoux, using Synchronized Chronology, also places the date of Herod's death in 1 BC. The two main camps for the date of the death of Herod are 4 BC and 1 BC.

Most scholars think that Jesus was born one or two years before Herod's death, given his order to kill male children under two years old. Luke mentions a census when Jesus was born, ordered by Caesar Augustus when Quirinius was governor of Syria. However, Quirinius was governor starting in 6 AD, well after Herod's death. Scholars have grappled with this inconsistency for centuries. Many scholars believe that was an error on the part of Luke. Some assert that there were multiple events that could be called a census in those times, and perhaps Luke got the wrong one. There are also theories proposed that the proper translation of the Greek written by Luke does not say Quirinius was *governor* of Syria. They assert that the word used was not the official title of the governor but a less specific word that encompasses broader governing roles, perhaps a previous position held by Quirinius.

There is much disagreement on these details and the dates, and much is written on these subjects. Based on a review of many sources, there appear to be two distinct camps: those who believe Jesus was born between 6 and 4 BC and those who believe he was born in 3 or 2 BC. The Catholic Church accepts that Jesus was born in 3 or 2 BC. The range 6 BC to 2 BC covers the most credible theories.

There is also general disagreement about what month and day Jesus was born. Some say that the descriptions of the shepherds in the fields tending their sheep rule out the winter as the time since sheep are not usually out in the fields at that time of year; however, others dispute that. Records of a comet in 5 BC, which could be the star mentioned, suggest it was visible between March and May. Various ancient writings from around the end of the second century place Jesus' birth on multiple dates. Clement of Alexandria in the *Stromata (c. 190 AD)* indicates that Jesus was born on November 17th or 18th, but he mentions that others place it on May 20th, April 19th, or April 20th. Theophilus of Antioch in the late second century and St. Hippolytus of Rome in the early third century placed Jesus's birth on December 25th. This is likely the source of that date being chosen. Another later writer, St. Epiphanius of Salamis, puts it on January 6th.

The early church chose December 25th as the date to celebrate the birth of Jesus and January 6th as the date of the epiphany (the visit by the Magi or wise men). The church does not claim December 25th to be the literal date of Jesus' birth. Frankly, we do not know what month and day Jesus was born; the Bible does not say, early writings conflict, and no records have been found that definitively give us that information.

One question that might come to mind is, "Isn't the current calendar supposed to start in the year of Jesus' birth?" Yes, that is true, but the BC/AD system, based on the birth of Jesus, was first proposed in 525 AD by Dionysius Exiguus, a Scythian monk. It is unknown how he established that Jesus was born 525 years prior. Scholars agree that he used incorrect information or simply made a mistake and was off by a few years. Given how difficult it must have been to research such things back then, over five hundred years later, being off by only a few years was pretty good.

This uncertainty about the actual year of Jesus' birth is part of why some people have adopted BCE (Before Common Era) and CE (Common Era) instead of BC and AD, which are based on the birth of Christ. However, the main reason is that non-Christians did not like using a system based on Jesus' birth.

Both the Gospel of Matthew and the Gospel of Luke describe the lineage of Jesus. Matthew 1:1-17 starts with Abraham, goes through to King David, and then through twenty-seven generations to Joseph. Luke 3:23-38 begins with Joseph and works backward through forty-two generations to King David, then back to Abraham, and back to Adam and Eve. The generations between King David and Joseph are different in the two Gospels, including even Joseph's father's name, with some convergences. The generations between Abraham and King David are the same in the two Gospels.

There are multiple theories to explain the differences. The difference in Joseph's father's name could be explained if Joseph's biological father died and his father's brother, through the practice of Levirate marriage, married his mother; it is possible that Joseph had two legal fathers. Joseph's grandfather's name is similar in both. Differences further up the line could be explained by tracing lineage through the male or female ancestor. Some scholars point out that when the female line was used, the male's name, as the son-in-law of the male/female ancestor pair, was listed as son.

Using that same logic, some scholars assert that Luke's ancestry is Mary's. Joseph was listed instead of Mary, as was the practice then. They say Joseph was the son-in-law of Heli, Mary's father. There are early writings not in the Bible, like the supposed Gospel of James, Jesus' brother, that list Mary's father as Joachim and her mother as Anne. Joachim is a variant of Eliacim, which is abbreviated Eli, which is a variant of Heli, which is listed in Luke's ancestry of Jesus as his grandfather. So, it is not clear if Luke was describing Jesus' ancestry through Mary. However, it is a popular theory,

My first thought on this was, why does Joseph's ancestry matter if Jesus is not Joseph's biological son? I understand that for Jesus to fulfill the prophecy related to the Messiah, he must be descended from David, but Joseph's ancestry does not prove that. However, some scholars suggest that in the same sense that Jesus can be described as the son, albeit adoptive, of Joseph, he can be described as of the house of David. That is a far simpler explanation.

If Mary was also of the house of David, then the prophecy would be fulfilled that way. There is another discussion of Mary's ancestry in Luke asserting that Mary was related to Elizabeth, the mother of John the Baptist, and that Elizabeth was decedent from Aaron, the brother of Moses, implying that Mary was as well. Some suggest that Mary was related to Elizabeth through her mother but that her father was descended from David.

The Catholic Encyclopedia says, *"It is granted on all sides that the Biblical genealogy of Christ implies a number of exegetical difficulties,"* and it mentions all the theories discussed above and asserts that most of these theories are possible and have not been disproven. However, it concludes that tradition holds that Mary was a decedent of David through Nathan. Scholars point out that it was common for people to marry within their clan, so Mary likely belonged to the house of David, whether Luke is describing Jesus' genealogy through Mary or not.

From my research, early Christians from the second century on believed that Mary was of the house of David as well as Joseph.

So, what can we conclude? It seems likely, or at least possible, that both Joseph and Mary were descended from David, given marriage practices at the time. Also, the statement that Jesus can be described as "of the House of David" through his adoptive father, Joseph, makes sense.

If, in over a thousand years of discussing this topic, none of the previously discussed theories about the differences in genealogies presented in Matthew and Luke can be proven or disproven, then we cannot be sure which theory is correct; however, we cannot rule them out either.

Detractors believe that both genealogies are false and are made up to support Jesus' fulfillment of prophecy. However, they have offered no proof of that assertion or any information to add to the discussion about Jesus' genealogy.

To be complete, we should consider the arguments made by non-believers that Jesus did not exist and that zealots made up the story of Jesus to support the creation of a new religion. From reading many sources, it is obvious that the people making those arguments ignore the eyewitness accounts in the Bible, the accounts in other books that were not included in the Bible, and the accounts by non-Christian historians like Flavius Josephus (AD 37 -100) and Cornelius Tacitus (AD 56 – 100) that mention Jesus and that confirm some of the details in the Bible like the crucifixion of Jesus by Pontius Pilate.

If Jesus were made up, it would have had to have been a massive conspiracy enlisting many people to create the historical record that we have today. There are many papers and books on this subject. From my research, the consensus is that Jesus existed in the first century, he was Jewish and was a Rabbi or teacher in Galilee, Judea, and the surrounding areas. His teachings are the basis of Christianity, and he was crucified by Pontius Pilate.

While belief in many of the things discussed in the gospels requires faith, the existence of Jesus and the basic facts of his life and crucifixion are widely accepted as historical facts.

The Early Life of Jesus

Summary

- Joseph and Mary fled to Egypt with Jesus to avoid Herod's slaughter of the innocents.
- They returned to Judea after Herod's death but decided to live in Galilee in the town of Nazareth, well away from Bethlehem and Jerusalem.
- Jesus had four brothers and at least two sisters.
- Jesus studied the Jewish religion and was a good student.
- Jesus learned to be a "carpenter" or "craftsman."
- Jesus probably worked as a craftsman once he reached adulthood and before starting his ministry.

- Around the age of 30, Jesus was baptized by John the Baptist, and God spoke his praise of Jesus.
- The devil unsuccessfully tempts Jesus, after which Jesus starts his ministry.

Discussion

There is not much information in the Bible about Jesus' early life up until he was around thirty. The Bible in Matthew 2 mentions that when Joseph and Mary learned Herod had ordered the killing of male children under two years old in and around Bethlehem, they fled to Egypt and stayed there until after Herod's death.

Some scholars doubt this story about Herod slaughtering the innocents, stating that such an event would have a more significant historical footprint. However, others point out that Bethlehem was not that big a place at the time. Estimates range from as small as three hundred people to a population of 1,000 to 3,000. Assuming the larger estimate, using current census data showing what percentage of the current population is male and 0-2 years old and factoring in the higher infant mortality rates, I came up with 10-30 male children in that age range. The website Catholic Answers lists numbers in this same range. While any number is horrific, it might not have been big news that the Romans killed that many children.

Joseph, Mary, and Jesus lived in Egypt until after Herod died. Various sources say they lived in Egypt for a few months to a couple of years, but we do not know for sure. They returned to Judea, but because Herod's son Archelaus was ruling in place of his father, they were afraid to return to Bethlehem, so they went to the region of Galilee to a town named Nazareth, where Jesus was raised. The Gospel of Matthew skips forward until Jesus is around thirty years old, telling us nothing else about Jesus' early life.

There is a story in Luke 2:41-52 about Jesus, who was twelve years old, going to Jerusalem for the feast of Passover with his parents. When it was done and they returned home, they did not realize that Jesus was not in the caravan. When they realized that he was not with them, they returned and searched for him. It took three days to find him in the temple, sitting with the teachers, listening to them, and asking questions. The teachers were astounded at his understanding. His parents were upset at him, and he said,

"Why were you looking for me? Did you not know that I must be in my Father's house." Luke 3:49 (NABRE)

This is the first time that Jesus implies that he is the son of God. Luke then ends the story with Jesus returning home and,

"He went down with them and came to Nazareth, and was obedient to them; and his mother kept all these things in her heart. And Jesus advanced in wisdom and age and favor before God and man." Luke 2:51-52 (NABRE)

Then, like Matthew, Luke jumps forward until Jesus is about thirty years old. Many authors attempt to fill in the missing details by describing what life was like in

Galilee and what his education might have been like. However, that is speculation.

There are a few other writings that describe the childhood of Jesus. The earliest is the *Infancy Gospel of Thomas*. Some scholars say that it is from the mid to late second century. The earliest reference to it is from Irenaeus of Lyon around AD 180, who calls it spurious and apocryphal. It appears to be a work of fiction designed to show the power of Jesus. I read some of it, but it read more like a story than an eyewitness account. It was clearly not written by Thomas, the disciple of Jesus. He was younger than Jesus and did not know Jesus as a child. He could not have witnessed the events described, nor would he have been alive in the mid-second century to write it. There are others written even later, but they are all considered speculative or fictional in nature, so they are not worth summarizing here.

We can infer some things about Jesus' childhood from various Bible passages. The story about Jesus in the temple when he was twelve tells us that Jesus was a skilled student of the Jewish religion. This is reflected in his knowledge of those teachings in his ministry.

Matthew recounts an event in Nazareth when Jesus came back there to teach,

"Where did this man get such wisdom and mighty deeds? Is he not the carpenter's son? Is not his mother named Mary and his brothers James, Joseph, Simon, and Judas? Are not his sisters all with us?" Matt 13:54-56 (NABRE)

This passage tells us that Joseph, Jesus' adoptive father, was a carpenter and that Jesus had four half-brothers and at least two half-sisters. So, he would have grown up as the oldest of at least seven children. Mark 6:2-6 recounts the same story, mentioning the identical brothers and sisters, but refers to Jesus himself as a carpenter,

"Is not this the carpenter, the son of Mary and brother of James and Joses and Judas and Simon? And are not his sisters here with us?" Mark 6:3 *(ESV).*

These passages, taken together, imply that Jesus was apprenticed to Joseph, his adoptive father, and learned to be a carpenter.

One aside here, the Catholic Church, the Eastern Orthodox church, and some Protestant denominations believe that Mary remained a virgin all her life. There is a vast amount written on this subject, and it is difficult to find any unbiased discussions about the subject.

To believe that Mary remained a virgin all her life, one must explain the passages in the Bible that infer that Mary does not remain a virgin and the passages that mention Jesus' brothers and sisters, and there are quite a few. The most direct passages are those from Matthew 13:54-56, and Mark 6:2-6 discussed above, explicitly mentioning and naming four brothers and some number of sisters more than one. Matthew, talking about Joseph, says,

"He had no relations with her until she bore a son, and he named him Jesus." Matt 1:25 (NABRE)

This could imply that they had relations after that but does not assert that they did. Luke says,

"And she gave birth to her firstborn son and wrapped him in swaddling clothes, …" Luke 2:7 (ESV)

The word firstborn possibly implies that Mary had other sons later. There is also a passage in Mark 3 where Jesus is teaching, and he is creating a stir. Mark says,

"And his mother and his brothers came, and standing outside they sent to him and called him. And a crowd was sitting around him, and they said to him, 'Your mother and your brothers are outside, seeking you.'" Mark 3:31-33 (ESV)

The proximity of Jesus' mother and brothers implies that they are brothers via Mary and not more distant relations. There is a similar account of this event in Matthew 12:46-47 and again in Luke 8:19. There is also a reference to Jesus' brothers in 1 Corinthians 9,

"Do we not have the right to take along a Christian wife, as do the rest of the apostles, and the brothers of the Lord, and Cephas?" 1 Cor 9:5 (NABRE)

and a reference to one of his brothers in Galatians 1,

"But I did not see any other of the apostles, only James the brother of the Lord." Gal 1:19 (NABRE)

Then there is also John 2, which says,

After this he went down to Capernaum, with his mother and his brothers and his disciples, and they stayed there for a few days." John 2:12 (ESV)

John 7 has another reference,

"So his brothers said to him, 'Leave here and go to Judea, so that your disciples also may see the works you are doing. No one works in secret if he wants to be known publicly. If you do these things, manifest yourself to the world.' For his brothers did not believe in him." John 7:3-5 (NABRE)

And finally, Acts 1 which says,

"When they entered the city they went to the upper room where they were staying, Peter and John and James and Andrew, Philip and Thomas, Bartholomew and Matthew, James son of Alphaeus, Simon the Zealot, and Judas son of James. All these devoted themselves with one accord to prayer, together with some women, and Mary the mother of Jesus, and his brothers." Acts 1:13-14 (NABRE)

The proponents of the theory of Mary's perpetual virginity assert that the brothers and sisters mentioned are Joseph's children from an earlier marriage. They claim that Joseph was much older than Mary and died when Jesus was young. We know that Joseph was still around when Jesus was twelve in the story about Jesus in the temple, and he was capable of making the journey. The Bible does not cover the eighteen years between that time and when Jesus was about thirty years old. Joseph is not explicitly mentioned after that but could be indirectly referenced in the statement *"Is not this the carpenter's son?"* discussed above, but that is inconclusive.

We do not know when Joseph died except that it was after Jesus was twelve. That certainly leaves time for Joseph and Mary to have children. While it could be the case that some or all of Jesus' brothers and sisters are from an earlier marriage, there are no scriptures that mention Joseph having been married before and having children before Jesus. Another proposal is that the Greek word used for brothers, "*adelphos*," might not mean biological brothers and sisters, but it could have a broader meaning that could include cousins. However, other scholars dispute that the word was used that way at that time in history. Yet another explanation is that these passages referred to his disciples. However, Acts 1:13-14, John 2:12, and John 7:2 all distinguish between the disciples and Jesus' brothers.

I understand that this is a sacred belief of the churches mentioned above. I looked for support in the Bible for this idea and in the writings of many of the proponents to see what they cite. The Bible clearly says that Mary was a virgin up to the time Jesus was born but does not assert it after that. Some people say that when Jesus, on the cross, asked John to care for his mother, John 19:26-27, it implies that Jesus did not have brothers and sisters as that duty should fall to them. But others point out that Jesus' brothers were not believers at that time, so he passed that duty to one of his closest followers. Both thoughts are conjecture.

I investigated the source of the belief in the perpetual virginity of Mary. It appears that it first came from the Gospel of James (~150 AD), which does assert this to be the case. The church rejected that gospel. It was not included in the Bible, and an early pope condemned it. However, the belief in Mary's perpetual virginity persisted and was accepted by many. The condemned Gospel of James is often cited, even today, in relation to this topic. Centuries later, the perpetual virginity of Mary became an official part of doctrine (Second Council of Constantinople in 553 AD, Lateran Synod in 649 AD). The Catholic Church says that it has been divinely revealed, and any other belief is heretical.

I am not going to take a position on Mary's perpetual virginity. I certainly understand why that belief is appealing, and I also understand why people think the Bible passages mentioned above contradict that belief. I am not sure that it is essential for our salvation that we believe one way or the other. Perhaps we can just remain aware of both points of view. I will leave it to the reader to decide what to believe.

Continuing the discussion of Jesus' early life, Luke, in the story about young Jesus at the temple, says,

"Each year his parents went to Jerusalem for the feast of Passover." Luke 2:41 (NABRE)

This implies they were a devout family. The picture emerges of Jesus, being raised in a big family with all that implies, diligently studying religion, and learning to be a carpenter from Joseph. Luke sums it up with,

"The child grew and became strong, filled with wisdom; and the favor of God was upon him." Luke 2:40 (NABRE)

Some scholars conjecture that once Jesus reached adulthood, he made his living as a carpenter. The statement mentioned above from Mark 6:3 certainly implies that is the case. Interestingly, some linguistic scholars point out that the original Greek word used could be translated as *"carpenter,"* *"craftsman,"* *"builder,"* or *"artisan."* Meaning it is possible they worked with wood and stone as required by the job, and indeed, some believe that he was a stonemason, not a carpenter. It seems likely that a *"craftsman,"* *"builder,"* or *"artisan"* would need to work with multiple mediums. We do not know that fine level of detail.

There are many stories and books written about the "lost years," the time in Jesus' life between the ages of 12 and 29. One such book claims Jesus traveled to India, Nepal, Ladakh, and Tibet as both a student and teacher, seeking knowledge and enlightenment at some point in those years. However, from what I can tell, there is broad agreement among scholars that the story is false.

We do not know anything about the so-called "lost years." The Bible is mainly about Jesus' ministry, teachings, and what his disciples, apostles, and followers did after that. The story of Jesus' life picks up again with a discussion of his relation to and interactions with John the Baptist, which marks the beginning of his ministry.

Matthew picks back up when Jesus was about thirty years old. He describes John the Baptist preaching in the desert of Judea. John does not claim to be the messiah but tells people to repent because the kingdom of heaven is at hand. He starts baptizing people in the Jordan River for repentance at the same time, telling people that someone mightier than himself is coming. Of course, the local Pharisees are not pleased.

Jesus shows up to be baptized by John, and John recognizes him and says that Jesus should be baptizing him. However, Jesus insists, and John baptizes him.

"After Jesus was baptized, he came up from the water behold, the heavens were opened for him, and he saw the Spirit of God descending like a dove and coming upon him. And a voice came from the heavens, saying, 'This is my beloved Son, with whom I am well pleased.'" Matt 3:16-17 (NABRE)

Matthew 4 goes on to discuss Jesus being forced to fast for forty days and forty nights and then being tempted by the devil. The devil tempts him three times, but Jesus resists each attempt. The devil gives up and leaves him having failed, and angels show up to minister to him. According to Matthew, this marked the beginning of Jesus' ministry.

What Did Jesus Look Like?

Summary

- Jesus is not described in the Bible. As far as we know, he looked like any average male Jew of limited means in Judea.
- The speculation is that he had brown eyes, dark brown to black, possibly curly, hair, olive skin, and was between five feet and five feet five inches tall.

Discussion

There has been a lot of speculation about what Jesus looked like. The Bible does not describe him. If Jesus' appearance was remarkable in any way, it would likely be mentioned. Given that, people assume that his appearance was unremarkable. When Judas betrayed Jesus and brought a crowd to arrest him, he told them he would kiss the one they were to arrest. One theory is that the crowd could not identify Jesus because he looked similar to his disciples. (Matt 26:47-49)

In the book *"What did Jesus Look Like?"* by Joan E. Taylor, she concluded that Jesus looked like most Jewish men in the area: brown eyes, dark brown to black hair, olive-brown skin, and roughly five feet five inches tall. Others suggest that he would have been a few inches shorter than that and that his hair was likely curly.

We do not know if he had a beard, but given that he roved around teaching, many speculate that it is likely. Jewish men depicted on Judaea Capta coinage (coins issued by the Romans to commemorate the capture of Judea) from that era had beards and medium-length or short hair. Some people point to 1 Corinthians 11:14-15, which indicates that a man wearing long hair is a disgrace. So, he may have had short or medium-length hair. He possibly had long sideburns and an untrimmed beard, given the Old Testament rules,

"You shall not round off the hair on your temples or mar the edges of your beard." Lev 19:27 (ESV)

For clothing, like most male Jews of limited means, Jesus probably wore a prayer mantle with tassels (shawl), knee-length wool or linen tunic or cloak, an inner garment like a shorter, thinner tunic, a belt, and sandals. John 19:23-25 describes the soldiers taking Jesus' clothes, dividing them among themselves four ways, and casting lots for his tunic. It describes a seamless tunic woven in one piece from the top. It is unclear if that is the inner or outer garment. The rest is not described. So, his garments could not just be rags, or the guards would not have wanted them.

This is all, at best, informed speculation. We do not know what Jesus looked like or what he wore.

Languages Known by Jesus

Summary

- It is likely that Jesus spoke Aramaic as his first language but also spoke Greek and Hebrew.
- He was able to read Hebrew, and possibly Aramaic and Greek.
- He may have been able to write.

Discussion

The primary languages spoken in the area where Jesus grew up were Aramaic and Greek for everyday speech and Hebrew for studying the Jewish religious texts. Luke 4:16 describes Jesus standing up in the synagogue to read from the scrolls. So, apparently, he could read Hebrew and likely other languages as well. Most scholars assert that Aramaic was his first language.

The Romans, who ruled the area, spoke Greek and Latin. Some scholars suggest that it was likely that Jesus also spoke Greek. There were Greek-speaking towns around Nazareth like Sepphoris (see *"Galilee: History, Politics, People"* by Richard A. Horsley), which was only four miles away, was the capital of Galilee and possibly the birthplace of his mother, Mary. Some point out that if Jesus was a carpenter and did work around the area, he would have needed to know both Aramaic and Greek.

Speaking Greek would also allow him to talk to Roman administrators. In Matthew 8:5-13 Jesus speaks with a Roman centurion, and in Matthew 27:11, Mark 15:2, Luke 23:3, and John 18:33-34 he speaks to the Roman governor Pilate. Scholars think that these conversations would have been in Greek. Jesus taught to people in areas outside of Judea where he may have needed to speak Greek or even other languages.

The Roman military also used Latin, but most scholars agree that it was unlikely that Jesus spoke much Latin, but it is possible.

It was less common for people in Jesus' time and area to be able to write. There is one passage in John 8 that says that when the Pharisees were questioning Jesus,

"...Jesus bent down and wrote with his finger on the ground." John 8:6 (ESV)

"And once more he bent down and wrote on the ground." John 8:8 (ESV)

I investigated the original Greek for this verse. In John 8:6, the term used is "κατέγραφεν" (*katagraphó or kategraphen*); in John 8:8, the term used is ἔγραφεν (*egraphen*). The various Lexicons say these terms mean to write but could also mean to trace or draw in outline. So, we cannot be sure if he was writing, and of course, we do not know what he was writing or in what language.

Some claim that Jesus is hinting back to an Old Testament passage,

"O LORD, the hope of Israel, all who forsake you shall be put to shame; those who turn away from you shall be written in the earth," Jer 17:13 (ESV)

So, they think Jesus was writing the names of the Pharisees in the earth, and they would understand the biblical reference and significance of his actions. That may be the case, but that is speculative.

Jesus, Iesus, Iesous, Yeshua, or Isho'?

Summary

- Jesus was probably called Yeshua (YEH-shoo-uh) in his time, which is close to Joshua in English today.
- Aramaic: Isho' (ee-sho)
- Hebrew: Yeshua (YEH-shoo-uh)
- Greek: Iesous (ee-ay-sooce' or yay-soos)
- Latin: Iesus (YAY-sus)
- English: Jesus (JEE-zuhs)

Discussion

There is a lot of disagreement among scholars about how Jesus would have said his name. As discussed in Chapter 4: Sources, the earliest versions of the New

Testament books that we have today were written in ancient Greek. The name used in the Greek text, shown below, for Jesus, transliterates to Iesous and is pronounced as ee-ay-sooce'. I looked at high-resolution scans of the earliest papyrus copies of the New Testament to see how Jesus' name was written. In all the papyri I examined, Jesus' name was written in Nomina Sacra, which are abbreviations of sacred names. There are several different forms using the first two letters, the first three letters, the first and last letter, or the first two and the last letter, all with a bar over them. In the image below, the first Nomina Sacra example is how it was written in Papyrus 1 from Matthew 1:1, dated to c. 250 AD. The second Nomina Sacra example below is used in many of the letters of Paul as recorded in Papyrus 46, dated c. 175-225 AD.

Ἰησοῦς   ΙΗΣΟΥΣ or ΙΗΣΟΥ   ΙΥ̅ ΙΗΥ̅

Modern Greek   Ancient Greek Uppercase   Nomina Sacra

Many scholars assert that Jesus is a common Hebrew name. In Hebrew, Jesus is written as shown below. This transliterates to Yeshua and would have been pronounced YEH-shoo-uh, or some scholars assert that it is Yehoshua pronounced Yea-HO-shoo-ah. They point out that the current name Joshua in English is closer to the original Hebrew than Jesus.

יֵשׁוּעַ   ישוע

Modern Hebrew   Ancient Hebrew

However, other scholars point out that Jesus is thought to have spoken ancient Galilean Aramaic as his first language. Jesus's name written in Syriac Aramaic is shown below, and it transliterates to Isho', which is pronounced ee-sho.

Isho' and Yeshua are not very similar to how we pronounce Jesus in English. The Greek Iesous sounds closer to the way we say Jesus in English than either of those. Scholars say that when the Greek was transliterated to Latin, it was represented as Iesus, which is pronounced YAY-sus, which is similar to the Greek version. When the Latin was translated into English, the I was changed to J, and we get Jesus, which is now pronounced Gees-us or JEE-zuhs. The majority of scholars say Jesus would have been called Yeshua, but there is no consensus on that.

Chapter 2: The Teachings of Jesus

This chapter discusses the main teachings of Jesus prior to the events leading up to his crucifixion and resurrection. Those are addressed in the next chapter. The preferred source of Jesus' teachings is the direct quotes of his words attributed to him in the Gospels. After that, the explanations of his teachings in the Gospels and Acts are a pretty direct source of what Jesus taught. When Jesus refers to an Old Testament verse or teaching, it makes sense to read that text to understand his teachings. Other discussions of his teachings in the letters of Paul make sense to examine, but not as the primary source. It is sometimes unclear if Paul is giving his opinion, describing a practice of the early church, or representing a specific teaching of Jesus in these letters.

Some people try to analyze every word, draw tiny inferences from the text, and ascribe deep meanings to those tiny inferences. There are a substantial number of such speculations. I do not think it makes sense to do that. It does not seem likely that Jesus filled his teaching with vague and hidden meanings. He wanted people to understand. So, I looked for direct and straightforward meanings in his teachings consistent with this book's intention to summarize his main teachings. I will leave it to other authors to seek and justify hidden meanings.

When Jesus does not address a topic and the disciples do not discuss it either, we must assume that the Old Testament teachings still stand. Jesus directly modified some Old Testament teachings and reaffirmed others. In some cases, his teachings are stricter than in the Old Testament, and in others, he relaxes the rules mentioned in the Old Testament.

You might think this should be a simple task; just read the Gospels and the other books in the New Testament and glean out teachings attributed to Jesus. It is more complex than that. First, there are, in some cases, multiple accounts of what Jesus said as remembered by different individuals. For example, there are two different versions of the Lord's Prayer, one in Matthew 6:9-13 and another in Luke 11:2-4. They are a little different. Which is correct? Or are they both correct? Perhaps when Matthew says, *"forgive us our debts,"* and Luke says, *"forgive us our sins [or trespasses],"* they mean the same thing. Maybe Jesus used a phrase that could be translated either way. Perhaps we need to merge the different versions to better understand what Jesus said.

Another complexity comes from the fact that Jesus sometimes taught in parables, which are stories with a moral or message. Sometimes, those parables mean different things to different people. Some people get the point, and others do not. It helps to understand them by reading the analysis of learned scholars about the possible meanings. I endeavored to do that, and when there are possible multiple meanings, mention them.

Consistent with this being a summary of Jesus' teachings, I stick to his main line teachings and try not to recount the same teaching multiple times in different ways as Jesus did. The Gospels recount Jesus' teachings to multiple distinct groups. He taught the same things to those groups, often in different ways, with different stories. So, I tried to reduce that repetition.

I approached this by first discussing a big topic of keen interest, Jesus' teaching on salvation. Believe it or not, this is quite a contentious subject. The Sermon on the Mount, as recounted in the Gospel of Matthew, is a rich source for Jesus' teachings. After discussing salvation, I started with the Sermon on the Mount and used the Gospel of Matthew as a guide to decide what order to present Jesus' teachings after that.

Salvation

Summary

- Faith in Jesus is required for salvation. This implies you believe:
  - God exists.
  - Jesus is the son of God.
  - Jesus died for our sins.
  - Jesus was resurrected and taken up to heaven.
- Jesus taught, and the disciples believed that baptism is also required.

- We must observe God's laws and specifically the Ten Commandments.
- Faith alone is not enough; we must also do the will of God to enter into the kingdom of heaven.
- Blasphemy against God will not be forgiven.

Discussion

One of the most important things people want to know when they think about religion is, "What do I need to do to go to heaven?" I'm sure that you have seen commercials on television asserting that "all you need to do is say this prayer," and they usually go on to assert that you just need to believe that Jesus is the son of God, that he died on the cross for your sins and ask him to come into your life. That is it; have faith in Jesus, and you get eternal life in heaven!

There are names for this theory. It is called "Substitutionary Atonement," "Vicarious Atonement," the "Atonement Theory," or "Substitution." There is also a variant named "Penal Substitution."

Substitutionary Atonement is the idea that humans have committed horrific sins, starting with the original sin in the Garden of Eden and many sins throughout our lives. The biblical punishment for sin is death and damnation. We are not worthy of going to heaven because we can never atone for all those sins. Substitutionary Atonement asserts that Jesus willingly, as an act of love for mankind, allowed himself to be crucified, and through that willing sacrifice, he took our place. Through that sacrifice and suffering, he atoned for the sins of mankind, including original sin and all past, present, and future sins, thus making it possible for humans to go to heaven. All we need to do to receive that gift is to have faith in Jesus.

Penal Substitution is a similar concept, with the difference being that it asserts that Jesus agreed to be punished for the sins of mankind and thus atoned for our sins. The difference is that Jesus either offered himself up in our place as a means of atonement, or he agreed to be punished for our sins instead of us. There is a lot of disagreement on this fine point. Some reject the thought that God would punish Jesus for sins he did not commit (Penal Substitution) but accept that God would allow Jesus to sacrifice himself in our place (Substitutionary Atonement), and others argue the opposite.

I am not sure if it matters which of these models we believe. It is clear from multiple places in the Bible that faith in Jesus is required for salvation. It is also clear that faith in Jesus means that we believe God exists, that we believe Jesus was the Son of God, that we believe Jesus died to atone for our sins, that we believe he was resurrected and ascended to heaven, and that we believe his teachings. Some scriptures are cited to support the Substitutionary Atonement view and others the Penal Substitution view, but as far as I can tell, it is not essential that we choose one of those views.

While I had never heard the terms Substitutionary Atonement or Penal Substitution before doing the research for this book, I was certainly barraged by that message growing up and the assertion that faith in Jesus is all that is required for salvation. I thought all

Christians believed that, but I discovered that many Christians do not believe faith alone is enough. In fact, the largest group of Christians on the planet, Catholics, and some Protestants, do not subscribe to that belief. They do believe that faith in Jesus is required to go to heaven, but they do not believe that is all that is required.

When I was a young teen, I began to question the belief that faith alone was all that was required to go to heaven. Something about it did not seem right to me. The thought that the worst mass murderers could, on their deathbeds, convert, declare faith in Jesus, and thus be forgiven and go to heaven, never having demonstrated their faith or atoned for their sins, just seemed unlikely to be true. I have felt uncomfortable with that concept ever since. I did not realize until recently that many Christians grapple with the same issue.

The assertion that salvation is achieved through faith alone came from the Protestant Reformation in the 16th century, attributed to Martin Luther and John Calvin. They did not create the idea, but they popularized the concept. People were tired of all the things the Catholic church said they had to do, of not being able to read the Bible for themselves, and of the excesses and abuses of the Catholic church, at that time, particularly the selling of indulgences. Luther's and Calvin's theories offered an uncomplicated way to salvation, and it quickly caught on, spurring the rise of Protestantism. That movement also spawned the so-called anti-reformation or counter-reformation in the Catholic church, where the church endeavored to purge itself of the abuses and practices that had brought about the Protestant Reformation and to heal the schism. They are still attempting to heal the schism today.

Rather than discuss the differences between what Catholics and various Protestant versions of Christianity believe, let us discuss what Jesus taught about salvation.

John recounts a conversation between Jesus and Nicodemus, a prominent Pharisee. He comes to Jesus, admitting that Jesus is a teacher from God and that no one can do the things that Jesus has done unless God is in him. Jesus says,

"Amen, amen, [Truly, truly] I say to you, no one can see the kingdom of God without being born from above. Nicodemus said to him, 'How can a person once grown old be born again? Surely he cannot reenter his mother's womb and be born again, can he?' Jesus answered, 'Amen, amen, [Truly, truly] I say to you, no one can enter the kingdom of God without being born of water and Spirit.'" John 3:3-5 (NABRE)

Jesus admonishes Nicodemus for not understanding, given that he is a religion scholar. Jesus ends up saying,

"And just as Moses lifted up the serpent in the desert, so must the Son of Man be lifted up so that everyone who believes in him may have eternal life." John 3:14-15 (NABRE)

This refers to the story in Numbers 21:4-9 where God had punished the people for complaining against God and Moses by sending serpents to bite them. They repented and asked Moses for help. He prays, and God instructs Moses to make a bronze serpent and raise it up on a pole, and anybody who looks at it would be saved from the punishment of serpent bites. It was an act of faith in return for salvation from the serpent bites. The obvious implication is that Jesus must be lifted up so people can look at him, have faith, and be saved. John goes on to summarize,

"For God so loved the world, that he gave his only Son, that whoever believes in him should not perish but have eternal life. For God did not send his Son into the world to condemn the world, but in order that the world might be saved through him. Whoever believes in him is not condemned, but whoever does not believe is condemned already, because he has not believed in the name of the only Son of God." John 3:16-18 (ESV)

Clearly, from these teachings, Jesus is saying that faith in him is required to have eternal life. The "being born of water and Spirit" part from John 3:5 is much debated. Almost universally, scholars think that being born of Spirit is the declaring faith in Jesus. Some scholars suggest that being born of water could mean human birth, the water referring to the amniotic fluid that surrounds a baby in the womb. However, others say the mention of being born again implies it is not that. I could find no evidence or references from the time that suggest that the phrase "born of water" was used to refer to birth. Other scholars suggest that it could refer to baptism. They refer to several passages in the Old Testament with baptism symbology. For example, the following passage:

"I will sprinkle clean water over you to make you clean; from all your impurities and from all your idols I will cleanse you. I will give you a new heart, and a new spirit I will put within you. I will remove the heart of stone from your flesh and give you a heart of flesh. I will put my spirit within you so that you walk in my statutes, observe my ordinances, and keep them." Ezek 36:25-27 (NABRE)

The thought is that Nicodemus, a religious scholar, should understand the *"born of water"* reference based on this and other references in the Old Testament.

There are many references in the New Testament about baptism. For example,

"Peter said to them, 'Repent and be baptized, every one of you, in the name of Jesus Christ for the forgiveness of your sins; and you will receive the gift of the holy Spirit.'" Acts 2:38 (NABRE).

Or in Acts 19 1:6, where Paul was talking to some disciples in Ephesus and asked them about their baptism. They tell him that John the Baptist baptized them. He lets them know that it is not the same as being baptized in the name of Jesus. He then baptizes them in the name of Jesus, and they then receive the holy spirit.

It seems clear that the writers of the New Testament believed that Jesus taught us that baptism was required as part of being born again. From my reading, the early church also interpreted it that way and saw baptism as necessary to wash away your sins. From what I can determine, the notion that baptism was an expression of faith but not required for salvation comes from the Reformation.

I was convinced by,

"Then Jesus approached and said to them, 'All power in heaven and on earth has been given to me. Go, therefore, and make disciples of all nations, baptizing them in the name of the Father, and of the Son, and of the holy Spirit, teaching them to observe all that I have commanded you'" Matt 28:18-20 (NABRE)

While it is not clear what happens to the souls of people who believe and are never baptized, it seems clear that Jesus taught that we should be baptized and observe his teachings.

Another teaching of Jesus that speaks about salvation comes from the Sermon on the Mount. In Matthew's retelling, Jesus talks about the commandments,

"Do not think that I have come to abolish the law or the prophets. I have come not to abolish but to fulfill. Amen, I say to you, until heaven and earth pass away, not the smallest letter or the smallest part of a letter will pass from the law, until all things have taken place. Therefore, whoever breaks one of the least of these commandments and teaches others to do so will be called least in the kingdom of heaven. But whoever obeys and teaches these commandments will be called greatest in the kingdom of heaven. I tell you, unless your righteousness surpasses that of the scribes and Pharisees, you will not enter into the kingdom of heaven." Matt 5:17-20 (NABRE)

This teaching of Jesus says that we must observe the commandments to be accepted into heaven. I was concerned when I first read the part about needing to be more righteous than the Scribes and Pharisees. I thought that was an extremely high bar. However, in other places in the Bible, Jesus makes it clear that he does not think highly of the Scribes and Pharisees, so perhaps this is just another dig at them and not such a high bar. The *"you will not enter into the kingdom of heaven part"* says to me that following the commandments is a requirement. Given that, it is hard to believe that somebody who has willfully, perhaps gleefully, broken the commandments in their life can, in their last moments, express faith in Jesus and be forgiven and go to heaven, never having done anything to demonstrate their faith and commitment to the commandments or to atone for their sins.

The concept of purgatory was likely born out of thoughts like this. People who have sincere faith but have not atoned for their sins or were good people but never had the opportunity to know Jesus, go to a place where they can atone in some way, and if they succeed, they go to heaven. However, I have not discovered any direct teachings of Jesus about purgatory. Catholics believe its existence is implied by several New Testament passages that may imply a place between heaven and hell or the possibility of forgiveness after death, such as 2 Timothy 1:18, Matthew 12:32 and 5:25-26, Luke 23:43, and 1 Corinthians 3:11–3:15. I hope they are correct, but there is at most a hint of such a place in those passages. They also mention some Old Testament passages like 2 Maccabees 12:38-45 that describe making atonement for the dead so that they could be absolved of their sin, implying that the souls are in a place where forgiveness is still possible. If you want to know more, there are articles and books about the biblical basis for purgatory. For example: *www.catholic.com/magazine/online-edition/is-purgatory-in-the-bible* and "*Purgatory Is for Real: Good News About the Afterlife for Those Who Aren't Perfect Yet,*" Karlo Broussard, 2020.

Finally, another teaching of Jesus in Matthew speaks directly about what is required for salvation. Jesus said,

"Not everyone who says to me, 'Lord, Lord,' will enter the kingdom of heaven, but only the one who does the will of my Father in heaven. Many will say to me on that day, 'Lord, Lord, did we not prophesy in your name? Did we not drive out demons in your name? Did we not do mighty deeds in your name?' Then I will declare to them solemnly, 'I never knew you. Depart from me, you evildoers.'" Matt 7:21-23 (NABRE)

It is clear that Jesus taught we need to have faith in him, but we must also endeavor to do the will of God. Those who claim to have faith in Jesus, do works in his name, and even preach his teachings, but who do not do the will of God do not go to heaven. To me, that implies following the commandments as well as learning about and attempting to follow other teachings of Jesus and of God from the New and Old Testaments. From this and the other teachings mentioned above, salvation from faith alone is not what Jesus taught.

Jesus also taught that there is one thing that can prevent you from going to heaven,

"Therefore I tell you, every sin and blasphemy will be forgiven people, but the blasphemy against the Spirit will not be forgiven. [32] And whoever speaks a word against the Son of Man will be forgiven, but whoever speaks against the Holy Spirit will not be forgiven, either in this age or in the age to come." Matt 12:31-32 (ESV)

He is saying that blasphemy against Jesus can be forgiven, but blasphemy against God will not be forgiven.

The Ten or Eleven Commandments

Summary

- There are eleven concepts mentioned in the descriptions of the commandments.
- Various sources represent, interpret, and number the commandments differently.
- Some of the commandments are represented in popular culture differently than they were written in the Bible.
- Jesus made it clear that we must follow these commandments.
- Read the list in the discussion below.

Discussion

As discussed in the previous section, according to Matthew 5:17-20, Jesus reaffirms the need to follow the commandments in the Sermon on the Mount. The statement captured in Matthew is clear,

"Therefore whoever relaxes one of the least of these commandments and teaches others to do the same will be called least in the kingdom of heaven, but whoever does them and teaches them will be called great in the kingdom of heaven." Matt 5:19 (ESV)

We are expected to follow the commandments and teach others to do the same. Further reinforcing the point, Jesus expounds at some length about a few of the commandments in Matthew 5:21-30. Let us first examine the commandments. If you are like me, when I tried to remember the Ten Commandments, I could not come up with all ten. Yet it is clear from both the New and Old Testaments that they are the law and the word of God. Given that Jesus specifically referred to and discussed the commandments, it is worth discussing them here.

The Bible lists the commandments in Exodus 20 and Deuteronomy 5. Exodus 20 describes what God said to Moses on Mount Sinai as follows (I added the numbering):

"And God spoke all these words, saying, I am the LORD your God, who brought you out of the land of Egypt, out of the house of slavery.
1. *You shall have no other gods before me.*
2. *You shall not make for yourself a carved image [idol], or any likeness of anything that is in heaven above, or that is in the earth beneath, or*

that is in the water under the earth. You shall not bow down to them or serve them, for I the LORD your God am a jealous God, visiting the iniquity of the fathers on the children to the third and the fourth generation of those who hate me, but showing steadfast love to thousands of those who love me and keep my commandments.

3. *You shall not take the name of the LORD your God in vain, for the LORD will not hold him guiltless who takes his name in vain.*

4. *Remember the Sabbath day, to keep it holy. Six days you shall labor, and do all your work, but the seventh day is a Sabbath to the LORD your God. On it you shall not do any work, you, or your son, or your daughter, your male servant, or your female servant, or your livestock, or the sojourner who is within your gates. For in six days the LORD made heaven and earth, the sea, and all that is in them, and rested on the seventh day. Therefore the LORD blessed the Sabbath day and made it holy.*

5. *Honor your father and your mother, that your days may be long in the land that the LORD your God is giving you.*

6. *You shall not murder [kill].*

7. *You shall not commit adultery.*

8. *You shall not steal.*

9. *You shall not bear false witness against your neighbor.*

10. *You shall not covet your neighbor's house.*

11. You shall not covet your neighbor's wife, or his male servant, or his female servant, or his ox, or his donkey, or anything that is your neighbor's."
Exod 20:1-17 (ESV)

Deuteronomy 5 describes Moses telling the people what God said on Mount Sinai. It is very similar and lists the same commandments with a bit more explanation in the one about the Sabbath.

You have no doubt noticed that I have listed eleven commandments in the list of the ten commandments. When I started reading the commandments in the Bible, I was struck by the fact that there are eleven concepts listed in the text of both Exodus and Deuteronomy. I immediately began to research this topic and discovered lots of discussion. It turns out that various sources represent, interpret, and number the commandments differently.

The Catholic, Lutheran, and Anglican Christian churches and the Jewish Talmud combine 1 and 2 above into a single commandment about having no other gods. They view the part about false idols to be further explanation of having no other gods. However, they believe this combined commandment forbids idolatry, superstition, spiritism, etc. Some other Protestants keep 1 and 2 split and combine 10 and 11 above into a single commandment about not coveting your neighbor's stuff, wife included. A friend of mine who is Catholic defended the split of 10 and 11, saying that they discuss two different sins, adultery and avarice. That is not a bad point, but Protestants point out that 1 and 2 are also two different sins, polytheism and idolatry, also not a bad point.

To me, there are clearly eleven concepts mentioned. All the variants of the Bible that I have read contain all eleven concepts. Yes, 1 and 2 are related, and yes, 10 and 11 are related. So, you could represent these as nine, ten, or eleven commandments as long as no concepts are omitted. I wondered why people insist that there are ten commandments.

It turns out that there is another apparent list of commandments discussed in the Bible, in Exodus 34. Moses is supposed to have smashed the original tablets when he found the people worshiping a golden calf, and God told Moses to cut new tablets and that God would write the same commandments again on those tablets. Moses cuts the blank tablets and takes them to God.

In a careful reading of Exodus 34, you will see that God told Moses a list of things and told Moses to write them down as a covenant that he was making with Moses and Israel,

"And the Lord said to Moses, 'Write these words, for in accordance with these words I have made a covenant with you and with Israel.'" Exod 34:27 (ESV)

It does not say that the statements in Exodus 34:10-26 are the commandments. God said that he would write the same commandments on the stone tablets as before. He clearly commands Moses to write down these other statements as a covenant. While three of the commandments are mentioned in these covenant statements, 1, 2, and 4, from the list above, the rest of the statements are different and talk about practices, festivals, and sacrifices that people should observe. The commandments written on the stone tablets by God and the statements in the covenant that Moses is supposed to write down appear to be two different things. However, there is a mention of "the ten words [commandments]" in Exodus 34:28 that led people to think there are ten commandments. By my reckoning, there are about fifteen distinct things that God commands mentioned in the discussion of the covenant. So, the commandments and the covenant are clearly not the same thing, but this statement in Exodus 34:28 likely led to people believe that there are ten commandments. Unfortunately, we do not have the stone tablets today to see how those commandments were organized.

I was also struck by the realization that the popular representation of some of the commandments alters the meaning, as stated in Exodus 20 and Deuteronomy 5. For example, I was taught that there was a commandment, *"Thou shall not lie,"* which seems like an overly broad interpretation of *"You shall not bear false witness against your neighbor."* Saying that you saw your neighbor do something or heard him say something that you did not see or hear would be bearing false witness. Telling someone you enjoyed a meal they prepared for you when you did not, is not bearing false witness against your neighbor. It is unclear that this commandment, as written in Exodus and Deuteronomy, forbids lying in all circumstances. I am not advocating lying; there are other passages in the Bible that make it clear that lying is a sin.

I am just pointing out that the commandment discusses a specific form of lying.

Similarly, I was taught that there is a commandment: *"Thou shall not kill."* In some translations of the Bible, it says *"kill,"* and in others, it says *"murder."* These are quite different meanings. Saying *"thou shall not kill"* implies that we cannot kill others under any circumstance. Saying *"thou shall not murder"* leaves room for killing in self-defense, in a war in defense of one's tribe, village, city, or country. This is a crucial difference, while murder is killing, all killing is not murder! I spent some time researching this topic and found a plethora of articles and books discussing that *"shall not kill"* is a mistranslation of a Hebrew phrase that is closer to *"shall not murder."* These articles also point out that in the Old Testament, there are places where God commands people to kill others, so *"thou shall not kill"* is not consistent with God's other commands (for example, Deuteronomy 20:16 and Samuel 15:3). Some articles point out that the Hebrew word used does not correctly translate to either kill or murder, but rather a concept like murder, but with a broader interpretation than the word murder. Some suggest the word used might include what we call murder and what we call manslaughter. For example, killing through neglect or even carelessness, but not self-defense, war, or accidents. There is a gray area there; it is best if we can avoid killing others, but perhaps "unjust killing" is what was intended.

Given that Jesus specifically emphasized the need to follow the commandments, it is important for our salvation that we understand each of them correctly and do our best to follow them.

The Greatest Commandments

Summary

- Love God with all your heart, with all your soul, and with all your mind.
- Love your neighbor as yourself.

Discussion

There is another story in Matthew where the Pharisees question and test Jesus. They ask him which commandment is the greatest. Jesus responds with,

"You shall love the Lord, your God, with all your heart, with all your soul, and with all your mind. This is the greatest and the first commandment. The second is like it: You shall love your neighbor as yourself. The whole law and the prophets depend on these two commandments." Matt 22:37-40 (NABRE)

Many sources assert that Jesus is adding a new commandment to love your neighbor. It is consistent with his other teachings, but it is not new. It comes from the Old Testament,

"You shall not take vengeance or bear a grudge against the sons of your own people, but you shall love your neighbor as yourself: I am the Lord." Lev 19:18 (NABRE)

Jesus was not creating a new commandment. He was reinforcing or elevating long-standing Old Testament teaching to the importance of a commandment.

The Sermon on the Mount

The Sermon on the Mount is recounted in detail in the Gospel of Matthew. It is a detailed sermon with many of Jesus' teachings, given early in his ministry. Luke recounts the Sermon on the Plain. It is similar to the Sermon on the Mount with many similar messages but shorter. Many scholars think they are the same sermon recounted differently and at different levels of detail by Matthew and Luke. Others think they are similar sermons given to different audiences. In the following sections, I describe the teachings mentioned in the longer Sermon on the Mount and note some differences from the Sermon on the Plain.

How should we live our lives?

Summary

- The Beatitudes lay out a prescription for a happy, Godly life. Jesus says we should willingly seek God's grace, seek comfort from God when we grieve, be meek, be merciful, thirst for righteousness, have a clean heart, be peacemakers, and trust that if we are persecuted for our faith, God will reward us.
- We should preserve God's and Jesus' teachings.
- We should not hide our faith but rather be a shining beacon on the hill, showing the way by our faith and deeds.

Discussion

Jesus opens the Sermon on the Mount with a set of sayings called the Beatitudes, which is thought to explain how we can live a good (Godly) life and achieve a state of happiness.

> *"Blessed are the poor in spirit,*
>   *for theirs is the kingdom of heaven.*
> *Blessed are they who mourn,*
>   *for they will be comforted.*
> *Blessed are the meek,*
>   *for they will inherit the land.*
> *Blessed are they who hunger and thirst for*
>   *righteousness, for they will be satisfied.*
> *Blessed are the merciful,*
>   *for they will be shown mercy.*
> *Blessed are the clean of heart,*
>   *for they will see God.*
> *Blessed are the peacemakers,*
>   *for they will be called children of God.*
> *Blessed are they who are persecuted for the sake of*
>   *righteousness, for theirs is the kingdom of heaven.*
> *Blessed are you when they insult you and persecute*
> *you and utter every kind of evil against you [falsely]*
> *because of me. Rejoice and be glad, for your reward will*
> *be great in heaven. Thus they persecuted the prophets*
> *who were before you."* Matt 5:3-12 (NABRE)

When I read these, the meaning of some is obvious, and others are not. I first thought, what does *"poor in spirit"* mean? It is not an expression in current use, and its meaning is not obvious. It does not sound good to be poor in spirit, so why are those who are, blessed? I sought out the analysis of others and found a few popular explanations. I briefly summarize these views below.

One view asserts that being poor in spirit is a realization that we are sinful and need God's love and guidance, and we, therefore, willingly seek God's grace. Such people are more likely to pray daily, seek God's guidance and forgiveness, and be mindful of God's word in good times and in bad. If that is the meaning, then it makes sense why such people would be blessed.

Another camp asserts that it means to be humble or "humble in spirit." To me, these two camps are making similar points. However, the word humble does not convey the same relationship to God that the other view does, but perhaps "humble in spirit" could imply the same concept, but it is less obvious. If we think our spirits are in great shape, we might not see the need for God, but if we are humble in spirit, we might admit that we need him and seek him.

Some others relate it to being poor in wealth since Luke's version says, *"blessed are you who are poor"* and does not say *"in spirit."* They explain that when you are poor, you concentrate on the necessities in life like food, water, clothing, and shelter, and you do not have time for other distractions. Someone who is poor in spirit and concentrates on the necessities of the spirit, like prayer, avoiding sin, doing good works, or being a good person and doing the will of God, is blessed.

These are similar thoughts, and they may describe what Jesus intended. I will leave it to you to decide what he meant, but I hope these descriptions help.

"Blessed are they who mourn" may not be obvious either. We all mourn at times for a loved one, a pet, a missed opportunity, an unwise decision, etc. Why would we be blessed for that? In general, it is thought to mean that if we have faith in God, and look to him for comfort when we grieve, we will be comforted. So, people who look to God in their time of grief will be blessed with comfort from God.

"Blessed are the meek" can be misinterpreted as well. Meek does not mean weak or cowardly. It means you are humble, patient, not easily provoked, not quick to anger, not a troublemaker, and you willingly submit to God's will. It does not mean you are weak or unwilling to defend your loved ones, country, or God.

In summary, the Beatitudes lay out a prescription for a happy, Godly life. Jesus is saying we should willingly seek God's grace, seek comfort from God when we grieve, be meek, be merciful, thirst for righteousness, have a clean heart, be peacemakers, and trust that if we are persecuted for our faith, that God will reward us.

Similes of Salt and Light

After the Beatitudes, Jesus says,

"You are the salt of the earth. But if salt loses its taste, with what can it be seasoned? It is no longer good for anything but to be thrown out and trampled underfoot. You are the light of the world. A city set on a

mountain cannot be hidden. Nor do they light a lamp and then put it under a bushel basket; it is set on a lampstand, where it gives light to all in the house. Just so, your light must shine before others, that they may see your good deeds and glorify your heavenly Father."
Matt 5:13-16 (NABRE)

Again, after reading the thoughts of others, the meaning that rang true to me is that salt preserves, and we should, as the salt of the earth, preserve God's and Jesus' teachings. Also, we should not hide our faith but rather be a shining beacon on the hill, showing the way by our faith and deeds.

Anger

Summary

- Do not stay angry with others. Instead, we should resolve our differences quickly.

Discussion

In Matthew 5:21-24, from the Sermon on the Mount, Jesus is reinforcing the commandment not to murder, and he discusses anger. He mentions that in addition to not murdering, we should not stay angry with others. We should resolve our differences quickly and do it before we come to the altar to pray. It also says we should settle our differences and debts with others lest they fester, and we end up in court and being thrown in prison.

"Settle with your opponent quickly while on the way to court with him. Otherwise your opponent will hand

you over to the judge, and the judge will hand you over to the guard, and you will be thrown into prison. Amen, I say to you, you will not be released until you have paid the last penny." Matt 5:25-26 (NABRE)

Some scholars suggest that there is also a deeper meaning here about settling with God for our sins by doing penance and that the prison could be purgatory, where we stay until we have done so. I will let the reader decide if it could mean that.

Adultery

Summary

- Do not commit adultery.
- Do not have lustful thoughts and think about committing adultery.

Discussion

In Matthew 5:27-30, from the Sermon on the Mount, Jesus reinforces the commandment not to commit adultery. Jesus goes further and says,

"But I say to you, everyone who looks at a woman with lust has already committed adultery with her in his heart." Matt 5:28 (NABRE)

Presumably, this applies to women lusting after men as well. He goes on to discuss plucking out your eye if it causes you to sin or cutting off your hand if it causes you to sin. Hopefully, those statements are metaphors, not literal, or most of us will have missing eyes and hands.

The meaning appears to be that we should avoid lustful thoughts. This is particularly difficult in our oversexualized world, where we are barraged daily with lurid images and videos of attractive people and depictions of adultery. However, Jesus is saying that we should do whatever is necessary to control our lustful thoughts. For example, do not look at pornography, watch movies with this content, or frequent places where things are going on that invoke such thoughts.

In case you are wondering, the original Hebrew word used in the Old Testament commandment is *"na'aph,"* which translates to adultery and refers to a married person having sex with someone other than their spouse.

That term is not used to apply to unmarried people having sex. The word for that is *"zana,"* which translates to fornication.

Marriage and Divorce

Jesus continues to discuss divorce in the Sermon on the Mount. Since they are related, I will cover his teachings about both marriage and divorce in this section.

Summary

- Marriage is between a man and a woman who are adults and not closely related.
- If you divorce, you must give your spouse a divorce certificate; you cannot just leave them and be divorced.

- In the eyes of God, a legal marriage, once consummated, is forever, and if you divorce and remarry, you are committing adultery.
- Marriage is unlawful in some cases.

Discussion

Marriage, as discussed in this section, refers to the religious practice of marriage, performed by a priest, minister, or rabbi and ordained by God. In current times, the term marriage is also used to describe a legally binding, non-religious civil union. Civil unions are not recognized by most churches as ordained by God.

Jesus' core teaching on marriage appears in multiple places in the New Testament and says,

"But from the beginning of creation, God made them male and female. For this reason a man shall leave his father and mother and be joined to his wife, and the two shall become one flesh. So they are no longer two but one flesh. Therefore what God has joined together, no human being must separate." Mark 10:6-9 (NABRE)

Almost identical words are found in Matthew 19:4-6 and Ephesians 5:31, and similar teachings are found in 1 Corinthians 7:10-11. These teachings reinforce Genesis 2, which says,

"That is why a man leaves his father and mother and clings to his wife, and the two of them become one body." Gen 2:24 (NABRE)

But it goes further in asserting that *"what God has joined together, no human being must separate."*

It is clear from this teaching that marriage, as ordained by God, is between a man and a woman, and we should not divorce.

There are other places in the New Testament that give advice about marriage. For example, in Paul's first letter to the Corinthians, 1 Corinthians 7:1-9 and in the Letter of Paul to the Ephesians 5:21-30. However, it is unclear how much of that is Jesus' teaching versus Paul's opinion. In both letters, he says that husbands and wives should be subordinate to each other. He indicates that we are not commanded to marry, but if we cannot control ourselves, we should marry and treat each other with respect. The Corinthians passage also indicates that unmarried people should not have relations, but that is the subject of another section.

In relation to divorce, the Old Testament says a man is allowed to divorce his wife if he finds in her something indecent, Deuteronomy 24:1. He just gives her a bill of divorce so she can prove it and dismisses her from his house. They were both then allowed to remarry. Jesus' teachings are stricter on marriage than the Old Testament rules. In Matthew, from the Sermon on the Mount, Jesus does allow divorce in one case; he says,

"It was also said, 'Whoever divorces his wife must give her a bill [certificate] of divorce.' But I say to you, whoever divorces his wife, unless the marriage is unlawful [except on the grounds of sexual immorality], causes her to commit adultery, and whoever marries a divorced woman commits adultery." Matt 5:31-32 (NABRE)

Much is written about the exceptive clause. The phrases *"unless the marriage is unlawful"* and *"for any reason except sexual immorality"* have different meanings. I looked to see what other translations of the Bible say, and most of them say sexual immorality, fornication, or unfaithfulness. It is only the Catholic versions that say, "unless the marriage is unlawful."

Catholic scholars postulate that Matthew was discussing behavior that occurred in the time between the marriage and the couple consummating their union, which could be as long as a year back then. Marriage could be dissolved back then if it was not yet consummated, as Joseph considered doing when he found that Mary was pregnant. Today, we use the term annulment to describe this situation. They also postulate that Matthew was referring to incestuous marriages or other illegal situations. Given that Mark, Luke, and other places in the New Testament do not include the exceptive clause, they do not believe it applies to a legal marriage after it has been consummated.

I researched what the oldest Greek versions of the New Testament say. Linguistic scholars say at the root of this statement was the Greek word *"porneia,"* which, at the time of Jesus, meant any form of illicit sexual intercourse, which included adultery, prostitution, pedophilia, homosexuality, lesbianism, fornication (sex between unmarried people), incest, and bestiality. Most scholars translated the Greek phrase *"me epi porneia"* to *"except on the grounds of sexual immorality"* or something similar.

If this is the correct translation, the most straight-forward interpretation is that Jesus is modifying the Old Testament teaching that a man could divorce his wife for almost any reason. He is changing it and is saying that divorce is allowed only if your wife (or the husband; the text could imply either one) engaged in any of these sexually immoral behaviors. After that, the woman cannot remarry, as any man marrying her would be committing adultery. It is unclear from this passage if the man was then free to remarry. However, other passages clarify this, Luke says that Jesus taught,

"Everyone who divorces his wife and marries another commits adultery, and the one who marries a woman divorced from her husband commits adultery." Luke 16:18 (NABRE)

Also, Mark 10 discusses a time when Jesus was teaching in Judea across the Jordan and says,

"And Pharisees came up and in order to test him asked, 'Is it lawful for a man to divorce his wife?' He answered them, 'What did Moses command you?' They said, 'Moses allowed a man to write a certificate of divorce and to send her away.' And Jesus said to them, 'Because of your hardness of heart he wrote you this commandment. But from the beginning of creation, God made them male and female. Therefore, a man shall leave his father and mother and hold fast to his wife, and the two shall become one flesh.' So they are no longer two but one flesh. What therefore God has joined together, let not man separate." Mark 10:2-12 (ESV).

Matthew 19:3-9 has a similar account. But it adds,

"The disciples said to him, 'If such is the case of a man with his wife, it is better not to marry.' But he said to them, 'Not everyone can receive this saying, but only those to whom it is given. For there are eunuchs who have been so from birth, and there are eunuchs who have been made eunuchs by men, and there are eunuchs who have made themselves eunuchs for the sake of the kingdom of heaven. Let the one who is able to receive this receive it.'" Matt 19:10-11 (ESV)

Taken together, these teachings are clear: you can divorce if one of you commits sexually immoral behaviors. However, neither of you can remarry, or you are committing adultery.

The Catholic translation indicates that divorce is only allowed in cases where the marriage was not legal in the first place. You could not validly marry a close relative, a child, someone of the same sex, someone who is already married, etc. God would not ordain such a marriage. Leviticus 18 in the Old Testament gives an extensive list of what is meant by a close relative. They contend that you cannot divorce even in the case of sexually immoral behaviors. See the discussion in *"Did Jesus Say Adultery Is Grounds for Divorce?"* Catholic Answers Magazine, Jimmy Akin, 7/1/2000.

Today, you can legally divorce for various reasons in the eyes of the government, but the Catholic church asserts that you are still married in the eyes of God and cannot remarry in the Church. However, they do allow annulment in various situations, as described later.

Some Protestant churches accept divorce, and some only accept it in the case of infidelity. Some allow remarriage in the church, but not in all cases.

While these teachings are widely ignored, like it or not, there are several clear implications drawn from this body of teachings. Marriage is between a man and a woman who are adults and not closely related. If you divorce, you must give your spouse a divorce certificate; you cannot just leave them and be divorced. In the eyes of God, a legal, consummated marriage is forever, and if you divorce and remarry, you are committing adultery.

One more point: the translation *"unless the marriage is unlawful"* has been more broadly interpreted than the original Greek phrase and is used to justify official annulment. In the Catholic church, if the marriage is declared unlawful, it can be annulled, and people can remarry. The criteria include being forced to marry, marrying under certain false premises, inability to understand what was going on like insanity, mental illness, or a lack of consciousness, your spouse deceiving you to get you to marry them, and several other circumstances. While many of those criteria seem reasonable as a reason to declare a marriage unlawful, it is not clear if Jesus had all that in mind.

Swearing Oaths

Summary

- Do not swear oaths by things in heaven or on earth.
- Let your yes mean yes, and your no mean no.

Discussion

In the Sermon on the Mount, Jesus mentions the Old Testament teaching about oaths,

"Again you have heard that it was said to your ancestors, 'Do not take a false oath, but make good to the Lord all that you vow.'" Matt 5:33 (NABRE)

In this teaching, Jesus may be referring to,

"You shall not swear falsely by my name, thus profaning the name of your God. I am the LORD." Lev 19:12 (NABRE)

Jesus modifies this by saying that we should not swear oaths by heaven or earth. At the time, it was common for people to swear by enduring things to give credibility to their oaths, like swearing an oath that as long as this mountain stands, I will do whatever. Swearing by God was the strongest possible oath. Jesus says we should not swear oaths in the name of things in heaven or on earth; instead,

"Let your 'Yes' mean 'Yes,' and your 'No' mean 'No.' Anything more is from the evil one." Matt 5:37 (NABRE)

You might ask, what about the practice of swearing to tell the truth in court or taking an oath to join the military or take public office? Does this teaching forbid this? Many scholars suggest that Jesus was referring to us making voluntary oaths on our own behalf, invoking God, heaven, or things on earth. However, they point out that it did not forbid taking oaths in general. Agreeing to take an official or formal oath or vow, and even invoking

God to witness the oath or help us keep the oath, is acceptable. Saying, *"I swear to tell the truth, the whole truth, and nothing but the truth, so help me, God,"* is different from saying, *"I swear in the name of God to tell the truth."* They assert that Jesus was saying that in our everyday life, we should not swear oaths on things in heaven or on earth. We should simply be true to our word. Perhaps thoughts like this are the origin of the saying, *"My word is my bond."*

Retaliation and Love of Enemies

Summary

- Do not retaliate or seek revenge for personal offenses.
- Do not fight people who think they have a legal claim on your minor possessions.
- Do not resist when you are forced to perform a service; instead, go the extra mile. This might create goodwill rather than create conflict.
- Be generous with people in need.
- Love your enemies and pray for them in hopes that they will see the light.

Discussion

In this teaching, Jesus mentions the Old Testament teaching,

"You have heard that it was said, 'An eye for an eye and a tooth for a tooth.'" Matt 5:38 (NABRE)

Meaning that we should retaliate in kind to injury, not by doing something more significant than the initial injury. Jesus modifies that to say that we should not retaliate,

"But I say to you, offer no resistance to one who is evil. When someone strikes you on your right cheek, turn the other one to him as well." Matt 5:39 (NABRE)

The consensus is that Jesus is teaching that we should not seek revenge or retaliate for personal offenses; we should let it go. Retaliation or revenge often results in escalation. It does not say that we should not defend ourselves or just allow ourselves to be killed. This teaching is talking about seeking revenge or retaliating. The next statement,

"If anyone wants to go to law with you over your tunic, hand him your cloak as well." Matt 5:40 (NABRE)

Tells us not to fight people who think they have a legal claim to some minor possession of ours; just give it to them. This agrees with the teaching mentioned in the teaching about anger, discussed above, about settling with your opponent rather than going to court and maybe ending up in prison. Back then, taking something to court could result in brutal "Roman justice." Jesus further says,

"Should anyone press you into service for one mile, go with him for two miles. Give to the one who asks of you, and do not turn your back on one who wants to borrow." Matt 5:41-42 (NABRE)

Back then, a Roman could grab you and force you to perform a service, like carrying something for a mile.

This teaching tells us to just do it and even go the extra mile, which might create goodwill instead of resisting and creating conflict. It also tells us to be generous to people in need. It is not telling us to allow ourselves to be enslaved or to give everything away.

Right after these teachings in the Sermon on the Mount, Jesus taught us that we should love our enemies,

"You have heard that it was said, 'You shall love your neighbor and hate your enemy.' But I say to you, love your enemies, and pray for those who persecute you, that you may be children of your heavenly Father, for he makes his sun rise on the bad and the good, and causes rain to fall on the just and the unjust." Matt 5:43-45 (NABRE)

This fits well with the previous teaching: love your enemies, do not seek revenge for personal offenses, do not fight with them over minor possessions, willingly perform a service, and be generous to people in need. Perhaps if we do that, by our example and through prayer for them, they might see the light and become children of the heavenly Father.

Almsgiving in Secret

Summary

- Almsgiving is the practice of giving food, money, clothing, or services to the poor.
- Do not do that for the purpose of receiving public praise, or the praise will be your reward rather than rewards from God.

Discussion

Almsgiving was the practice of giving food, money, clothing, services, time, and other considerations to the poor. Jesus encouraged this practice and the practice of performing righteous deeds in general. However, he made it clear that we should not do so to receive public praise. We should do it in secret for the right reasons, and God would reward us for that.

"Take care not to perform righteous deeds in order that people may see them; otherwise, you will have no recompense from your heavenly Father." Matt 6:1 (NABRE)

"But when you give alms, do not let your left hand know what your right is doing, so that your almsgiving may be secret. And your Father who sees in secret will repay you." Matt 6:3-4 (NABRE)

Does this mean that if people learn of your generosity, it is a problem? Probably not, it clearly says do not do it for the purpose of receiving public praise. If you do, your reward is that public praise, not a reward from God.

How to Pray

Summary

- Do not pray in public for the purpose of receiving public praise. If you do, that praise is your reward instead of a reward from God.

- When you pray, God knows what you need before you ask; you can just pray the Lord's prayer.

Discussion

Like the teaching on Almsgiving, in the Sermon on the Mount, Jesus taught that we should not pray in public for the purpose of receiving public praise. If you do, your reward is that praise instead of a reward from God. Instead, we should pray in private.

Does this mean that Jesus is saying that we cannot pray with others or in church? Probably not; the meaning is clearly not to pray in public for the purpose of receiving public praise.

He also taught that when we pray, we do not need to babble on, thinking that God will hear us better if we say many words. Instead, Jesus assures us that God knows what we need before we ask and tells us to pray like the example he gives, the Lord's Prayer.

There are two versions of the Lord's prayer in the Bible, one in Matthew 6:9-15 and another in Luke 11:2-4 and there are different translations with minor differences. Most churches use the one in Matthew because the one in Luke is shorter. The traditional words used in many churches come from Matthew in the King James Version KJV, with minor changes, and are:

Our Father who art in heaven,
hallowed be thy name.
Thy kingdom come,
Thy will be done
on earth, as it is in heaven.

Give us this day our daily bread,
and forgive us our trespasses,
as we forgive those who trespass against us,
and lead us not into temptation,
but deliver us from evil.
[For thine is the kingdom, and the power, and the
glory, forever.]
Amen.

Eastern Orthodox and some Protestant churches add the last line before Amen, but it is not part of the prayer used by Catholics; however, the congregation says a similar statement later in the mass. That line is in the KJV translation; however, it was not in the oldest Greek versions and is not in most of the current English translations. It is thought to come from the Didache, an early Christian instruction manual. This is an example of text added in KJV that was not part of the original text.

Also, some churches use the more literal translation of Matthew 6:12: "*and forgive us our debts, as we forgive our debtors*" instead of "*and forgive us our trespasses, as we forgive those who trespass against us.*"

It is not likely important which translation we use. Jesus' point was that God knows what you need, so you can just pray a prayer like this, and he will understand. One thing to note is that Mathew 6:8 says God knows "*what you need,*" which may be different than "*what you want.*"

There are many bible discussions about the Lord's Prayer, exploring if this is the only prayer we should say or need to say. Many bible scholars think that Jesus gave us this prayer as an example of how to pray, not as a prescription to say just those words. There is almost unanimous agreement that saying this prayer alone is adequate, but we are not limited to just that prayer. God knows what we need no matter what we pray. However, Jesus does not forbid us from saying other prayers. Jesus does entreat us to keep it short and to the point when he says,

"In praying, do not babble like the pagans, who think that they will be heard because of their many words. Do not be like them." Matt 6:7-8 (NABRE)

Fasting

Summary

- When you fast, do not look gloomy and neglect your appearance so that others will know you are fasting. Appear normal, and God will know you are fasting.
- Jesus did not instruct us to fast at any specific times.

Discussion

In Jesus' time, fasting could take the form of abstaining from certain types of food and drink or abstaining from food and drink all together and was used to express grief or to humble yourself before God. For example, Daniel 10:2-3 mentions that he was mourning and fasted for three weeks by not eating delicacies and meat, or drinking wine.

People fasted as part of the observance of various holy days and festivals and after tragedies. However, that was Jewish custom; it was not a practice dictated by the Torah except on the Day of Atonement, Yom Kippur, mentioned in Leviticus 23:27-28.

In a similar theme to almsgiving and public praying, Jesus taught that when you fast, you should not go around looking gloomy and neglecting your appearance so that other people will see that you are fasting. You should act normal so people do not know if you are fasting, but God will know and reward you. Matthew 6:16-18

Fasting is not that common in Christianity today. Since it was common in Jewish tradition, and since Jesus was Jewish, that is likely why he addressed this topic. Some Christians fast on special days, like Ash Wednesday, Good Friday, before receiving communion, etc. Some people give up some favorite food during Lent as a sign of devotion. Some Christians abstain from meat, dairy products, and alcohol on Fridays; some just refrain from eating meat on Fridays. Those fasts are all church traditions; Jesus did not instruct us to fast at any specific time.

Christians view that the Day of Atonement was replaced by Jesus atoning for our sins through the crucifixion. Given that, we do not need to have a particular day of atonement. However, some Christians do observe that day and fast. As far as I can tell, Christians are allowed to do so if they like.

Wealth

Summary

- Do not stockpile wealth for wealth's sake. You may come to value it more than God.
- Instead, stockpile riches in heaven by doing God's will, following his commandments, and doing good works in his name.
- This does not prohibit saving and making prudent investments for the future to provide for yourself and your family.

Discussion

This is a topic of interest to most people. Here is Jesus' teaching from the Sermon on the Mount,

"Do not store up for yourselves treasures on earth, where moth and decay destroy, and thieves break in and steal. But store up treasures in heaven, where neither moth nor decay destroys, nor thieves break in and steal. For where your treasure is, there also will your heart be." Matt 6:19-21 (NABRE)

Jesus also taught,

"Take care to guard against all greed, for though one may be rich, one's life does not consist of possessions." Luke 12:15 (NABRE)

In Luke 12, there is the Parable of the Rich Fool, who, faced with a rich harvest, decided to tear down his barns and build bigger ones to save it all and live the good life for many years. Jesus says,

"But God said to him, 'You fool, this night your life will be demanded of you; and the things you have prepared, to whom will they belong?' Thus will it be for the one who stores up treasure for himself but is not rich in what matters to God." Luke 12:20-21 (NABRE)

There is a lot of discussion about these teachings. Does this mean that we should not save for the future? The consensus is that it does not imply that. Right from the beginning of the Bible, there is a story in Genesis 41 where the Pharaoh in Egypt has a dream that he cannot interpret. He turns to a Hebrew slave, Joseph, to help him understand the dream. Joseph confirms that the dream means that God was warning of seven years of famine and that the Pharaoh should collect up and save food while abundant so people would not perish during the famine. This story is not about stockpiling wealth for wealth's sake but about planning for the future.

Other places in the New Testament make this clear,

"And whoever does not provide for relatives and especially family members has denied the faith and is worse than an unbeliever." 1 Tim 5:8 (NABRE)

So, prudent saving and investing for the future is not necessarily the same as stockpiling treasures. Jesus appears to be talking about stockpiling wealth well beyond what you need for the future. Worldly treasures are temporary, and amassing them could cross over into greed and materialism; stockpiling treasures in heaven is forever. Jesus said,

"No one can serve two masters. He will either hate one and love the other, or be devoted to one and despise the other. You cannot serve God and mammon [riches]." Matt 6:24 (NABRE)

The main point is that if we amass worldly treasures, we will begin to value them more than anything else, even God. It is better to amass goodwill with God than earthly treasures. We do this by doing God's will, following his commandments, and doing good works in his name. For example, giving alms to the poor with our excess wealth. So, if we end up wealthy, then we should do good things with that wealth. There is a story in Matthew 19 where a wealthy young man approaches Jesus. The young man asked him what he needed to do to gain eternal life. Jesus tells him to follow the commandments. He says that he has and wants to know what else he should do,

"Jesus said to him, "If you wish to be perfect, go, sell what you have and give to the poor, and you will have treasure in heaven. Then come, follow me." Matt 19:21 (NABRE)

The rich man leaves, sad, because he has many possessions.

"Then Jesus said to his disciples, 'Amen, I say to you, it will be hard for one who is rich to enter the kingdom of heaven. Again I say to you, it is easier for a camel to pass through the eye of a needle than for one who is rich to enter the kingdom of God.'" Matt 19:23-24 (NABRE)

The message is clear that people who become rich run the risk of worshiping their wealth and possessions more than God. Given all the abovementioned teachings, Jesus is not saying that it is evil to be rich. But you imperil your soul if you worship that wealth. Also, he indicates that doing good works with that money is an excellent way to build up treasures in heaven.

Dependance on God

Summary

- Stop worrying and trust in God.
- Use the skills God gave you to support yourself and help others.

Discussion

After the teaching on riches in the Sermon on the Mount, Jesus goes on to say:

"Therefore I tell you, do not worry about your life, what you will eat or drink, or about your body, what you will wear. Is not life more than food and the body more than clothing?" Matt 6:25 (NABRE)

And he continues with a discussion of how God provides for the birds in the sky and the plants in the fields. We should trust that he will provide for us as well.

"But seek first the kingdom of God and his righteousness, and all these things will be given you besides. Do not worry about tomorrow; tomorrow will take care of itself. Sufficient for a day is its own evil." Matt 7:33 (NABRE)

Some people, upon reading this, think it means we should stop working, give away everything, and just spend time worshiping God and assume he will provide. I admit, when I first read it, I was put off. I stopped reading the Bible for a while to think. My observation is that when people do that, they end up poor, homeless, hopeless, they lose their faith, and die an early death. There are people and organizations that do try to provide for such people; I donate to some of them myself, but if we all stopped working, who would provide?

Recently, a couple of thoughts about this occurred to me: when Jesus says that God will provide, maybe he does not mean that God will literally produce food, clothing, and shelter. He could mean that God will provide by giving us the tools we need to support ourselves, like the ability to learn skills, intelligence, and ability in some area or another. If we work and apply ourselves, we will have what we need. If we still find ourselves in trouble, God also provides by making it clear to believers that giving to the poor is a good thing. Maybe Jesus was telling us not to obsess over food and possessions or what will happen tomorrow and to make sure we first pay attention to doing God's will but also use the gifts God gave us to provide for ourselves and help others.

I started reading the thoughts of bible scholars and other writers and looking for other teachings to understand these. Many scholars suggest that the focus of this teaching is telling us not to worry about earthly necessities and to trust in God. Nowhere in this passage does it say that we should not work; the focus is all about worry that distracts us from doing God's will.

Some passages that seem to relate are,

"The thief must no longer steal, but rather labor, doing honest work with his own hands, so that he may have something to share with one in need." Eph 4:28 (NABRE)

"In fact, when we were with you, we instructed you that if anyone was unwilling to work, neither should that one eat." 2 Thes 3:10 (NABRE)

"Nevertheless we urge you, brothers, to progress even more, and to aspire to live a tranquil life, to mind your own affairs, and to work with your own hands, as we instructed you, that you may conduct yourselves properly toward outsiders and not depend on anyone." 1 Thes 4:10-12 (NABRE)

"In every way I have shown you that by hard work of that sort we must help the weak, and keep in mind the words of the Lord Jesus who himself said, 'It is more blessed to give than to receive.'" Acts 20:35 (NABRE)

These New Testament passages and many in the Old Testament make it clear that we are supposed to work to support ourselves. Indeed, it is thought that Jesus worked as a carpenter until he began his ministry around the age of thirty. Then, he worked diligently to spread God's word. So perhaps the scholars are correct; maybe these teachings simply mean we should stop worrying to the point of distraction and trust in God.

Judging Others

In the Sermon on the Mount, Jesus said,

"Stop judging, that you may not be judged. For as you judge, so will you be judged, and the measure with which you measure will be measured out to you. Why do you notice the splinter in your brother's eye, but do not perceive the wooden beam in your own eye? You hypocrite, remove the wooden beam from your eye first; then you will see clearly to remove the splinter from your brother's eye." Matt 7:1-5 (NABRE)

This one is clear: stop judging others and deal with your own faults before criticizing other peoples' faults. Once you have done that, you may see more clearly.

Pearls before Swine

In the Sermon on the Mount, Jesus said,

"Do not give what is holy to dogs, or throw your pearls before swine, lest they trample them underfoot, and turn and tear you to pieces." Matt 7:6 (NABRE)

The consensus is that Jesus is telling us not to waste time preaching to people who are not interested in hearing and who may even hurt us for trying.

The Answer to Prayers

Summary

There are multiple interpretations,
- Keep praying for God's love, guidance, and wisdom, and seek the kingdom of God, and you will be let in.

- Pray for whatever you want, but know that God will not give you things that harm you or somebody else. The answer may be "no" or different from what we requested.
- Pray for things that are consistent with the will of God, and your prayers will be answered.

Discussion

In the Sermon on the Mount, Jesus said,

"Ask, and it will be given to you; seek and you will find; knock and the door will be opened to you. For everyone who asks, receives; and the one who seeks, finds; and to the one who knocks, the door will be opened." Matt 7:7-8 (NABRE)

This teaching seems to indicate that we should pray; our prayers will be answered, and God will give us what we ask for. God does not just give us anything we ask for, so it cannot mean that.

Many think this refers to praying for God's love, guidance, and wisdom and seeking the kingdom of God, not material things. They assert that anyone who seeks God and asks to join his kingdom will be allowed in. So, we should keep praying, seeking, and knocking on heaven's door, so to speak, and we will be let in.

Others think this teaching includes asking for just about anything. It does not say we will get what we asked for, just that our prayers will be heard and answered, but the answer we receive might be "no" or different from what we asked for. For example, if we pray for something that will harm us or somebody else or if we pray for things that will violate other peoples' free will, the answer may be no.

Some also point out this clarification in the first letter of John,

"If we ask anything according to his will, he hears us." 1 John 5:14 (NABRE)

The implication is that we must ask for things that are consistent with the will of God. However, we do not know God's larger plan. So, just ask, and if what you ask for is consistent with God's will, he will hear you and answer in some way. That implies we must strive to understand God's will and pray for that. As the Lord's Prayer says, *"thy will be done on earth as it is in heaven."*

These all seem like valid interpretations.

The Golden Rule

In the Sermon on the Mount, Jesus said,

"Do to others whatever you would have them do to you." Matt 7:12 (NABRE)

Jesus indicates that we should treat others as we would like to be treated. Of course, the assumption is that we want others to treat us well.

The Narrow Gate

Summary

- Take the narrow path to salvation instead of following others to your destruction.

Discussion

Jesus taught in the Sermon on the Mount,

"Enter through the narrow [straight] gate; for the gate is wide and the road broad that leads to destruction, and those who enter through it are many. How narrow the gate and constricted the road that leads to life. And those who find it are few," Matt 7:13-14 (NABRE)

The consensus on this teaching is that Jesus is telling us there are two paths that we can follow in life. The wide gate and road that most people follow, or the narrow gate and road that leads to salvation. The gate symbolism may refer to using the wide gate in Jerusalem so that everybody will see how holy you are as you come to the temple, as opposed to using another gate since we are not supposed to seek public praise for what we do to worship God.

Whether the gate symbolism means that or not, scholars assert that Jesus is saying the road to salvation is narrow in that there are strict requirements that we must follow. The wide gate and road that allows you to do whatever you want will not lead to salvation. This teaching also asserts that few will follow the narrow road.

Some scholars assert that the origin of the phrase "the straight and narrow," meaning the honest and moral way of living, is from this teaching. Some translations say "straight gate" rather than "narrow gate," which is likely the origin.

False Prophets

Summary

- Be on your guard and look for the signs that a prophet, preacher, politician, or leader is true before we follow or support them.

Discussion

Jesus taught in the Sermon on the Mount,

"Beware of false prophets, who come to you in sheep's clothing, but underneath are ravenous wolves." Matt 7:15 (NABRE)

This one is clear: watch out for false prophets who seem nice but are really after something other than your salvation, like your money or your virtue. Jesus says we can recognize them by "their fruits," which could include the people who follow them, the things they do or do not do, their choices, and how they spend their time and your money. For example, preachers who seem holy on Sunday but who live lavish lifestyles, do not do God's will, and who break the commandments. There are many examples of people like this, and many people are fooled into following them until they see the bad fruits.

Unfortunately, when people realize they are following a false prophet, it can shake their faith in general and make them further compound their error by turning away from God. This could also apply to politicians and other leaders. So, we should be on our guard and look for the signs that a prophet, preacher, politician, or leader is true before we follow or support them.

Following Jesus' Teachings

Summary

- Listen to Jesus' words and follow his teachings to lay a solid foundation with God in heaven. If you ignore his words, it is to your peril.

Discussion

At the end of the Sermon on the Mount, Jesus said that listening to and following his teachings will help us build a solid foundation with God.

"Everyone who listens to these words of mine and acts on them will be like a wise man who built his house on rock." Matt 7:25 (NABRE)

If we do that, when the rain falls and the wind and floods come, the wise man's house still stands.

"And everyone who listens to these words of mine but does not act on them will be like a fool who built his house on sand" Matt 7:26 (NABRE)

If we do that, when the rain falls and the wind and floods come, the fool's house collapses and is ruined. Clearly, Jesus is saying to listen to his words and follow his teachings to lay a solid foundation with God in heaven.

Association with Sinners

After Jesus called Matthew, the tax collector, to follow him,

"And as Jesus reclined at table in the house, behold, many tax collectors and sinners came and were reclining with Jesus and his disciples. And when the Pharisees saw this, they said to his disciples, 'Why does your teacher eat with tax collectors and sinners?' But when he heard it, he said, 'Those who are well have no need of a physician, but those who are sick [do]. Go and learn what this means: 'I desire mercy, and not sacrifice.' For I came not to call the righteous, but sinners." Matt 9:9-13 (ESV)

The implication is clear: Jesus needs to be around people who need his help. This teaching does not indicate that people, in general, should spend all their time with known sinners but does imply that people wanting to pass on what Jesus taught might need to spend some time with such people.

Teaching to Resistant People

Summary

- If people do not want to hear his teachings, leave them alone.

Discussion

When Jesus saw that there were many people in need of his teachings, he gave the disciples the power to cure the sick and raise the dead, and he sent them out in pairs to do good works and spread his teachings. He also instructed them to avoid people who did not want to hear the teachings,

"And if anyone will not receive you or listen to your words, shake off the dust from your feet when you leave that house or town. Truly, I say to you, it will be more bearable on the day of judgment for the land of Sodom and Gomorrah than for that town." Matt 10:14-15 (ESV).

Jesus' Parable of the Sower in Matthew 13 is thought to make the same point. Sow your seeds in fertile ground, which means spreading your teachings to those who are receptive. However, Jesus' parables of the Mustard Seed and Yeast in that same section could imply that even the smallest teaching can have a significant impact. The teaching mentioned above about casting pearls before swine is also a similar point.

Jesus continued, letting them know that they could be persecuted for spreading his teachings,

"Behold, I am sending you out as sheep in the midst of wolves, so be wise as serpents and innocent as doves. Beware of men, for they will deliver you over to courts and flog you in their synagogues," Matt 10:16-17 (ESV).

Jesus concludes his instructions with,

"and you will be hated by all for my name's sake. But the one who endures to the end will be saved." Matt 10:22 (ESV).

Making it clear that they should persevere even in the case of adversity. This point supports his earlier teaching in the Sermon on the Mount in the Beatitudes.

Peace on Earth and Conditions of Discipleship

Jesus makes it clear in Matthew 10:34-36 that he is not here to bring peace on earth. He indicates that his teachings will set people against each other. He goes on to explain that his disciples need to love God more than their families and follow him, Matt 10:37-39. In another section, Matthew recounts Jesus teaching that our true families are those who do the will of God, Matt 13:50. He tells them that if they die for his sake, they will receive eternal life. Then, he sends them out to spread his teachings.

Working on the Sabbath

Summary

- Jesus loosened the rules for the Sabbath. It is okay to prepare and eat food and to do good works on the Sabbath while still keeping the day holy.
- Many Churches today go further than that and allow exceptions for family needs, and some lift the restrictions almost completely.

Discussion

Jewish tradition, based on the Old Testament, forbids working on the Sabbath, even preparing food, or cleaning up. Jesus was going through a wheat field with his disciples on the Sabbath, and they were hungry. He allowed them to pick and eat grain. The Pharisees saw this and confronted them. Jesus points out that priests work on the Sabbath and are held innocent, so should his disciples be held innocent. He comes across a man with a withered hand in the synagogue, and he asks if it is lawful to heal on the Sabbath. He asks if you had a sheep and it fell in a pit on the Sabbath, would they not pull the sheep out? He then heals the withered hand.

Jesus is making it clear that the prohibition to not do any work on the Sabbath does not make sense. In Mark's version of the same story, he quotes Jesus as saying.

"The Sabbath was made for man, not man for the Sabbath." Mark 3:27 (ESV)

This is thought to mean the Sabbath was intended to help people, not burden them more. He implies that the Pharisees were violating the Sabbath by imposing strict rules that made it a burden. So, Jesus is loosening the rules for the Sabbath. It is okay to prepare and eat food and to do good works on the Sabbath while still keeping the day holy, but the Pharisees hated him for it.

Today, churches still advise resting on Sunday and going to church or attending mass, but as the Catholic Catechism says, "Family needs or important social service can legitimately excuse from the obligation of Sunday rest. The faithful should see to it that legitimate excuses do not lead to habits prejudicial to religion, family life, and health." (CCC 2185) Some churches say people should avoid servile labor on the Sabbath, which may be what Jesus intended.

Some scholars assert that Paul's statement,

"Therefore let no one pass judgment on you in questions of food and drink, or with regard to a festival or a new moon or a Sabbath." Col 2:16 (ESV)

Frees us from the rules about observing the Sabbath or at least being judged for not observing those rules. Others think that is a far looser interpretation than Jesus intended. They think Jesus wanted to lessen the burdensome requirements but still expected people to rest and keep the day holy.

Jesus Teaching in Parables

As recorded in Matthew, Jesus often taught in parables, which are stories that illustrate a point. Matthew 13 recounts a time when Jesus went out and sat by the sea. A large crowd gathered around him, so he got into a boat and spoke to the crowd on the shore. He spoke at length but only in parables. The disciples asked him why he is teaching in parables, and he said,

"Because knowledge of the mysteries of the kingdom of heaven has been granted to you, but to them it has not been granted. To anyone who has, more will be given and he will grow rich; from anyone who has not, even what he has will be taken away. This is why I speak to them in parables, because 'they look but do not see and hear but do not listen or understand.'" Matt 13:11-13 (NABRE)

Jesus is saying that he is teaching by telling stories in hopes that it will help people to better understand his teachings. While the understanding of his teachings has been granted to the disciples, who will grow rich in spirit, that understanding has not been granted to others. By providing a story that illustrates the point, those willing to learn might understand. However, for those not open to learning, the parable will make no sense; they hear but do not listen or learn.

Matthew points out that teaching in parables fulfills a prophecy in Isaiah. Matthew recounts some of the parables.

Parable of the Sower and others

This section covers the parables of the Sower, Wheat, Mustard Seed, and Yeast

Summary

- Only receptive people will understand and retain Jesus' Teachings; we cannot reach everybody.
- There is evil in the world; we cannot root it all out, but God will sort it out in the end, not us on earth.
- A small teaching can have great results; even though Jesus' following started small, it will grow large and spread.
- Jesus' teachings will spread and grow and help us rise to heaven.

Discussion

Jesus tells the Parable of the Sower about sowing seeds on a path, on rocky soil, in thorns, and in rich soil. People do not understand, so he explains it. When we spread his teaching, some seeds will fall on the path where they will not grow, which is like people who hear but do not understand. Some seeds will fall on rocky ground where they start to grow but fail to take root, which is like people who initially embrace the teachings but forget about them when tough times come. Some seeds will fall into the thorns and be choked out, which is like people who hear the teachings, but their anxieties and the lure of money cause them to ignore the teachings. Some seeds will fall on fertile soil, grow, and bear fruit, which is the people who hear, understand, and embrace his teachings. The message seems to be that not everyone will accept and retain his teachings, just the people who are receptive.

He goes on to tell the parable of the wheat, saying that even when you spread the seeds on fertile ground, our enemy, the devil, will come and sow weeds. You cannot necessarily recognize the weeds or rip them up without damaging the crop, so let both grow. Then, let God separate them at the harvest and burn the weeds. This is thought to mean that there is evil in the world, and we cannot stamp it all out, but in the end, God will separate the good from the bad.

Jesus tells another parable about a mustard seed.

"The kingdom of heaven is like a mustard seed that a person took and sowed in a field. It is the smallest of all the seeds, yet it is the largest of plants when full-grown. It becomes a large bush, and the 'birds of the sky come and dwell in its branches.'" Matt 13:31-32 (NABRE)

Meaning that even a small teaching can have great results and that even though Jesus' following started small, it will grow large and spread.

Then he tells another parable about yeast,

"The kingdom of heaven is like yeast that a woman took and mixed with three measures of wheat flour until the whole batch was leavened." Matt 13:33 (NABRE)

A small amount of yeast can make a large amount of bread rise. Jesus' teachings are like that yeast; they will spread, grow, and help us rise to heaven.

Parables of the Hidden Treasure

Jesus tells more parables about the value of his teachings,

"The kingdom of heaven is like a treasure buried in a field, which a person finds and hides again, and out of joy goes and sells all that he has and buys that field. Again, the kingdom of heaven is like a merchant searching for fine pearls. When he finds a pearl of great price, he goes and sells all that he has and buys it." Matt 13:44-46 (NABRE)

This is thought to mean that his teachings are a treasure that we should seek or a pearl of great price that we should value above all things.

Parable of the Fishing Net

Jesus continues with another parable about what happens at the end,

"Again, the kingdom of heaven is like a net thrown into the sea, which collects fish of every kind. When it is full they haul it ashore and sit down to put what is good

into buckets. What is bad they throw away. Thus it will be at the end of the age. The angels will go out and separate the wicked from the righteous and throw them into the fiery furnace, where there will be wailing and grinding of teeth." Matt 13:47-50 (NABRE)

At the end, the good will be separated from the evil, and the evil will be cast into hell. This may also be where the concept of hell being like a fiery furnace came from.

Treasures New and Old

Jesus gives the people one last parable after they say that they understand his teachings,

"Then every scribe who has been instructed in the kingdom of heaven is like the head of a household who brings from his storeroom both the new and the old." Matt 13:52 (NABRE)

This is thought to mean that people who have learned Jesus' teachings and who understand them should be able to spread his teachings and help people understand them, as well as the Old Testament teachings that have been there all along.

Parable of the Lost Sheep

At another time, Jesus tells a parable about a shepherd with one hundred sheep. When one goes astray, he will leave the ninety-nine and search for the lost one. When he finds it, he will rejoice. Jesus says God is the same way; he does not want to lose anyone, Matthew 18:10-14.

Parable of the Prodigal Son

Summary

- Those who remain faithful to God will have great reward in heaven.
- Those who stray but realize the error of their ways, repent their sins, and return to God will be accepted into heaven with open arms.

Discussion

Luke 15 includes a parable about a man with two sons. The younger son comes to him and tells him that he does not want to wait for his inheritance; he wants it now. So, his father gave it to him. The son then takes it, goes to a foreign land, and squanders it in sinful (prodigal) pursuits. The son finds himself poor and hungry, working on a farm tending swine. He finally comes to his senses and realizes that his father's servants were far better off than he was and that he would be better off if he went back to his father, admitted his sins, and became a hired worker for his father. So, he goes back to his father to do just that. His father sees him coming from a far distance and rushes out to greet him. The son tells his father that he has sinned against heaven and him and that he no longer deserves to be called his father's son. His father orders the servants to bring the finest robes, puts a ring on the son's finger, and sandals on his feet. Then, he orders the servants to prepare a feast to welcome his lost son home.

The older son, who had been out working in the field, came to the house and heard the sound of music and dancing, and he asked one of the servants what was going on. The servant tells him that his brother has returned and that his father had ordered the feast to celebrate. The older son becomes angry and refuses to enter the house. The father came out to plead with him to come in. The older son points out that he had served the father all his life and had never disobeyed him. Yet his father had never given him a feast. Yet when his brother returns after squandering his inheritance on sinful pursuits, he gets a big feast. The father reminds him that everything he has will go to the older son and that he ought to be happy that his brother, who was lost, is now found, Luke 15:11-32.

There are multiple possible lessons in this parable. Some may see it as a story about how nice guys finish last. The younger son goes away, squanders his inheritance, sins against heaven and his father, yet gets a feast when he finally realizes the error of his ways. The older son, who had been faithful all along, never got such a feast. However, if you examine the story a bit deeper, you will realize that the older son's reward will be much greater than a feast. He will inherit everything his father has.

The consensus on this parable is that it is a story of redemption. If you think of the father as God and the sons as his people. It is clear that those who remain faithful to God will have great rewards in heaven. However, those who stray but realize the error of their ways, repent their sins, and return to God will be accepted into heaven with open arms. It is also a reminder to the faithful who never stray that great reward awaits them in heaven for their faithfulness.

There is another possible message in this parable for earthly parents. Do not make the mistake of giving all your attention to the problematic child and forget to praise and recognize the child who does what they are supposed to do and never causes trouble. Doing so could ultimately anger and alienate the good child.

A Lesson About Generosity

Jesus tells another parable about workers in a vineyard, which I will summarize. A landowner goes out at dawn and hires some laborers to work in his vineyard. He goes out again at nine o'clock, finds laborers in the marketplace standing around idle, and hires them as well. Then again at noon and three o'clock and hires more. He comes to the market again at five o'clock, finds others standing around idle, and asks them why. They say it is because no one has hired them. So, the landowner hires them as well. Later in the evening, he goes to the vineyard and tells the foreman to summon the laborers and pay them, starting with the last to arrive and ending with the first to arrive. He pays them each full day's wages no matter how long they worked. The people who were there all day are upset, saying they should get more. He admonishes them and points out that he is not cheating them; they were paid the wages they were due. He asks them if they are envious because he is generous. Matt 20:1-15.

One message in this story is that we should not be envious if somebody is generous with their money. If we were paid what we are owed, who are we to take issue with the generous person? However, the last will be first, and the first will be last implication in the story is thought to mean that Jesus is saying that anyone who believes in him and does God's will be saved just the same, whether that person comes to it earlier or later in life.

Giving to the Poor and Beggars

Summary

- Jesus taught that we should give generously to the poor but leaves it to us to decide how, when, and how much to give.

Discussion

I expected to find many teachings of Jesus on this subject based on how often I have heard ministers and priests talk about it. However, I was surprised that it does not appear to be one of Jesus' more frequent teachings. The Old Testament directs us to give the poor in several places. For example,

"The land will never lack for needy persons; that is why I command you: "Open your hand freely to your poor and to your needy kin in your land." Deut 15:11 (NABRE)

"Give alms from your possessions. Do not turn your face away from any of the poor, so that God's face will not be turned away from you." Tob 4:7 (NABRE)

"Whoever is generous to the poor lends to the LORD, and he will repay him for his deed." Prov 18:17 (ESV)

Some people assert we should give money to every beggar we encounter without judging. Pope Francis said much the same thing in 2017. Supporters of this idea often quote Jesus from the Sermon on the Mount,

"Give to the one who asks of you, and do not turn your back on one who wants to borrow." Matt 5:42 (NABRE).

However, that statement is taken out of context. It is in Jesus' teaching about retaliation and is discussing dealing with people who think they have a claim on something of yours. It is not clear if that section has anything to do with giving to the poor.

There are other teachings where Jesus clearly discusses giving to the poor. As mentioned earlier, Jesus teaches that when we give alms to the poor, we should not do so to receive public praise. Evidently, Jesus was expecting that we would give alms to the poor, Matt 6:2-4. I mentioned in a previous section about Jesus telling a rich man that if he wanted to be perfect, he could sell his possessions and give to the poor, Matt 19:21.

In Matthew 24, when Jesus is teaching about the final judgment at the end of days, he says he will say to the faithful people,

"'Come, you who are blessed by my Father, inherit the kingdom prepared for you from the foundation of the world. For I was hungry and you gave me food, I was thirsty and you gave me drink, I was a stranger

and you welcomed me, I was naked and you clothed me, I was sick and you visited me, I was in prison and you came to me.' Then the righteous will answer him, saying, 'Lord, when did we see you hungry and feed you, or thirsty and give you drink? And when did we see you a stranger and welcome you, or naked and clothe you? And when did we see you sick or in prison and visit you?' And the King will answer them, 'Truly, I say to you, as you did it to one of the least of these my brothers, you did it to me.'" Matt 25:34-36 (ESV)

This teaching makes it clear that Jesus sees helping the needy as a virtue. I could not find any teachings that explain how we should do that. Should we give to beggars directly, to churches that care for the poor, to charitable organizations that help the poor, should we pick a needy person or family and truly help them improve their situation? Should we donate our time and talents or tangible goods like food and clothing instead of or in addition to our money? I found this passage helpful,

"Each one must give as he has decided in his heart, not reluctantly or under compulsion, for God loves a cheerful giver." 2 Corinthians 9:7

I concluded that Jesus taught that we should give generously to the poor but left it to us to decide how, when, and how much to give. Every person is different with different means, and every situation is different. Use your own judgment related to giving. God will know if we gave generously or not and if the people we give to are genuinely needy or scamming us.

Fortunately, today, there are reputable, local, national, and global organizations to which we can donate our money, tangible goods, and our time to feed and clothe the poor, help with housing, medical needs, drug and alcohol rebab, education programs, job placement, etc. And there are organizations that audit them and help us determine which of them are most reputable.

The Blindness of Familiarity

Matthew recounts a story where Jesus returns to his hometown of Nazareth and teaches in the synagogue there. The people are amazed and say,

"'Where did this man get this wisdom and these mighty works? Is not this the carpenter's son? Is not his mother called Mary? And are not his brothers James and Joseph and Simon and Judas? And are not all his sisters with us? Where then did this man get all these things?' And they took offense at him. But Jesus said to them, 'A prophet is not without honor except in his hometown and in his own household.'" Matt 13:54-57 (ESV)

The message is that familiarity with a person can blind us and that we should not assume that people we know in our mundane lives are incapable of remarkable things.

Luke 4:16-29 recounts a similar story with the same message. Some people think it is another description of the same incident, and some think it is a different time that he taught in Nazareth, but the message appears to be the same in those passages.

God's Commandments vs. Tradition.

Matthew describes an event where some Pharisees and Scribes came and asked Jesus why his disciples broke the traditions of the elders (different from the laws of Moses). They give as an example that his disciples do not wash their hands before eating bread. Jesus turned it around on them and asked why they broke God's commandments. He says,

"And why do you break the commandment of God for the sake of your tradition? For God said, 'Honor your father and your mother,' and 'Whoever curses father or mother shall die.' But you say, 'Whoever says to father or mother, 'Any support you might have had from me is dedicated to God, so for the sake of your tradition you have made void the word of God.'" Matt 15:2-6 (ESV)

The Pharisees had the tradition of abandoning their parents and giving everything to their synagogues and their order. If their parents needed help, they would say, "Sorry, I gave everything to the church," or some such. That violates the commandment from God to honor your mother and father. He was demonstrating that the Pharisees were hypocrites and valued tradition over the word of God.

The disciples point out to Jesus that the Pharisees took offense. He says,

"Every plant that my heavenly Father has not planted will be rooted up. Let them alone; they are blind guides. And if the blind lead the blind, both will fall into a pit." Matt 15:13-14 (ESV)

Thus making it clear that the Pharisees are blinded by their traditions to the true will of God. Jesus is teaching us not to be bound by old traditions that are not from God but instead by his commandments and the will of God. He concludes that eating with unwashed hands does not defile. He is not suggesting that washing your hands is not a good idea; he is just saying that God does not command it.

The Sign of Jonah

The Pharisees and Sadducees come to Jesus to test him, and they demand a sign from heaven to prove that he is the Messiah. He admonishes them, saying,

"You know how to interpret the appearance of the sky, but you cannot interpret the signs of the times. An evil and adulterous generation seeks for a sign, but no sign will be given to it except the sign of Jonah." Matt 16:3-4 (ESV)

He refuses to give them a sign, saying they would not know how to interpret it. The sign of Jonah refers to the fact that Jonah was swallowed by the whale and brought out three days and nights later by God, thus foretelling his death and resurrection. He may also be saying that they will not know how to interpret that either.

The Leaven of Pharisees and Sadducees

In the subsequent passages, he warns the disciples to beware of the Leaven of the Pharisees and Sadducees. They think he is talking about the fact that they have no bread. He admonishes them for thinking that, and then they realize he is talking about their teachings.

Jesus does not think that the Pharisees and Sadducees faithfully represent the teachings of God. So that could apply today as a warning for us to be careful about believing the teachings of apparently faithful people who may not be correctly representing the teachings of God. This possibly reinforces the earlier teaching to beware of false prophets.

The Coming of Elijah or The Transfiguration

Matthew 17 recounts a story where Jesus takes Peter, James, and John, his brother, up a mountain. He is transfigured, and his face shines like the sun, his clothes turn white, and Moses and Elijah appear, and God speaks from heaven,

"This is my beloved Son, with whom I am well pleased; listen to him." Matt 17:5 (NABRE)

They are afraid and prostrate themselves. Jesus tells them to get up, and they are alone with Jesus. On the way down the mountain, he tells them not to discuss their vision until after he is gone. They ask him why the scribes say Elijah must come before the Messiah. Jesus says,

"Elijah will indeed come and restore all things; but I tell you that Elijah has already come, and they did not

recognize him but did to him whatever they pleased. So also, will the Son of Man suffer at their hands." Matt 17:11-12 (NABRE)

Matthew says, later in that section, they realize that Jesus is talking about John the Baptist, who had been imprisoned by the Pharisees and Sadducees and beheaded by the Romans by that point. And again, he is foretelling his demise at their hands when they do not recognize him as the Messiah either.

The Greatest Disciple

Summary

To be the greatest in the eyes of God, stop trying to be considered first and be last, serve others, be humble, and put others' needs above your own.

Discussion

One time, when Jesus and his disciples were going to Capernaum, the disciples were discussing among themselves who was the greatest disciple. When they got to the place they were going, Jesus asked them what they had been discussing, and none of them wanted to say. Jesus called them together, and he said,

"If anyone would be first, he must be last of all and servant of all." Mark 9:35 (ESV)

This means to be the greatest disciple in the eyes of God, stop trying to be considered first and be last, serve others, be humble, and put others' needs above your own.

A little later, James and John, the sons of Zebedee, ask Jesus to be seated to his left and right in heaven. He asks them if they are willing to go through what he is about to go through in reference to his coming crucifixion, which they clearly do not understand. They assure him they are. Jesus says,

"to sit at my right hand or at my left is not mine to grant, but it is for those for whom it has been prepared." Mark 10:40 (ESV)

There is much debate about the meaning of this, with widely varying opinions. To me, it means that Jesus will not arbitrarily grant those positions to James and John. Those positions are prepared for whoever earns them. However, if you just read the rest of the section, it says,

"But whoever would be great among you must be your servant, and whoever would be first among you must be slave of all. For even the Son of Man came not to be served but to serve, and to give his life as a ransom for many." Mark 10:43-45 (ESV)

It is the same message: do not seek to be first; be the servant of the other disciples or the slave of all if you want to be considered first and sit by Jesus in heaven.

What to do if your brother sins against you

Summary

- If your brother sins against you, try first to work it out with him and get him to repent and make recompense. Only start to escalate if that fails.
- Be as forgiving with others as God is with us.

Discussion

Matthew describes Jesus' teaching about what to do if your brother sins against you. In this context, brother is thought by many scholars to imply brother in faith, not just your actual blood relations. Jesus said that if your brother sins against you, you should first try to work it out with him (get him to repent the sin and make recompense). John's account makes it clear that if he repents, you should forgive him. If that does not work, take one or two witnesses to the sin with you and try again. If that does not work, tell the church and let the church try. If he will not listen to the church either and repent, then treat him like a Gentile or Tax Collector, Matt 18:15-18.

This makes it clear that you should first try to work it out in private. If that does not work, bring one or two witnesses to the sin and try again, in hopes that once confronted by those witnesses to the sin, it will help the brother recognize his sin. If that does not work, involve the church or the authorities. If your brother is still unrepentant, then exile or shun him. Some also think that if there are no witnesses to the sin, you cannot take the accusation beyond trying to work it out in private. They say this reconfirms Old Testament teaching from Deuteronomy 19:15. However, it is not clear if Jesus intended that if there are no witnesses, we should not involve the church. Another implication here is to try to get the brother to repent with the least amount of public embarrassment. Also, there was no separation of church and state back then, so today, it might mean going to the church and/or the legal authorities as appropriate based on the nature of the sin.

After this, Peter asks an obvious question. He asks how many times he should forgive his brother, as many as seven times, he asks. Jesus says not seven but twenty-seven times. And he tells a parable, which I will summarize. In the story, a man owes his king a considerable debt he cannot pay. So, the king decides to sell him, his family, and all his property to pay the debt. The man falls to his knees, gives homage to the king, and asks him to be patient, and he will pay the debt. Out of compassion, the King forgives the debt. Then, the man whose debt was forgiven encounters another man who owes him a much smaller amount. He demands payment, and when the second man also asks for time to pay back the debt, the first man refuses and has him put in prison. People observe this and tell the king. He calls the first man back and is angry that he did not show the second man the same mercy that was shown to him and hands him over to the torturers until he pays back the debt, Matt 18:21-34.

The message is clear: God is forgiving a vast number of sins for those who repent; we are expected to be similarly forgiving. However, it is also clear from this teaching that repentance is required for forgiveness. We are not instructed to simply forgive our brother's sins against us if our brother does not repent.

The Gospel is for Jews and Gentiles

A non-Jewish woman comes to Jesus and asks him to cast out a demon from her daughter. He does not respond at first, but she persists. His disciples want to drive her away, but Jesus says,

"'I was sent only to the lost sheep of the house of Israel.' But she came and knelt before him, saying, 'Lord, help me.' And he answered, 'It is not right to take the children's bread and throw it to the dogs.' She said, 'Yes, Lord, yet even the dogs eat the crumbs that fall from their masters' table.' Then Jesus answered her, 'O woman, great is your faith! Be it done for you as you desire.' And her daughter was healed instantly." Matt 15:23-28 (ESV)

This is thought to show that Jesus was testing the woman to see if she really had faith or just hoped he could heal her daughter. He takes her persistence and reverence as signs that she did and heals her daughter. Therefore demonstrating that Gentiles, as well as Jews, could receive his teachings.

Jesus the Messiah and Performing Miracles

Some scholars assert that Jesus did not claim to be the Messiah or the Son of God. That is not true, according to the Gospels. People also question if Jesus performed miracles. The Gospels are full of descriptions of the miracles that he performed. These two topics are interrelated, and both are discussed in this section.

Summary

- In numerous places in the gospels, Jesus is quoted as implying he is the Messiah and stating that God is his father. He often refers to himself as the Son of Man, which some scholars assert means he is the Messiah.

- All four Gospels, Matthew, Mark, Luke, and John, describe Jesus performing miracles to prove that he is the Messiah and the Son of God.

- Jesus tells a woman he meets in Samaria at Jacob's well that he is the Messiah.

- When Jesus is put on trial, he admits directly that he is the Messiah and the Son of God.

Discussion

The first time that Jesus says that God is his father is when he is twelve years old and is missing. As discussed earlier in the section on Jesus' early life, he is found in the temple talking to the teachers and asserts that it is his father's house.

Once his ministry started, the first person to assert that Jesus was the Son of God and the Messiah was John the Baptist, as described in John 1:29-34 after he baptized Jesus. Two of John the Baptist's followers, Andrew and John, hear this and start following Jesus. Andrew goes and finds his brother Simon Peter and tells him that he has found the Messiah (John 1:41), and he becomes the third disciple. Jesus then went to Galilee and met Philip, and Jesus called him to follow him. Philip finds Nathanael and tells him that he has found the Messiah. He meets Jesus and decides to follow him.

At this point, Jesus has five disciples, and they think he is the Messiah.

Jesus attends a wedding in Cana, and he invites his disciples to come along. At the wedding, they run out of wine, and Jesus' mother, Mary, asks him to help. Jesus ends up converting water into wine. This is the first miracle that the disciples witness, and John 2:11 says they start to believe.

There are several instances where Jesus makes it clear that he is the Messiah but is not quoted as saying those exact words. For example, in the discussion with Nicodemus, a Pharisee, discussed in the section on salvation. Nicodemus says that he knows Jesus is a teacher who came from God, based on Jesus' works to that point. In that discussion, Jesus implies three times that he is the Messiah. The third time, he uses the term "Son of Man" and says that everyone who believes in him may have eternal life.

In many places, Jesus describes himself as the Son of Man. It is much debated, but many scholars assert that the term Son of Man implies that he is both human and the Messiah. In the book of Daniel in the Old Testament, the term is used to describe the prophesied messiah,

"I saw in the night visions, and behold, with the clouds of heaven there came one like a son of man, and he came to the Ancient of Days (God) and was presented before him. He was given authority, glory and sovereign power; all nations and peoples of every language worshiped him. His dominion is an everlasting dominion that will not pass away, and his

kingdom is one that will never be destroyed." Dan 7:13-4 (ESV)

Jesus evidently assumed that people would understand the reference to prophesy. Jesus describes himself as the Son of Man around eighty times.

The first direct confirmation, using the term Messiah, is described in John 4. Jesus confirms that he is the Messiah to a woman whom he meets in Samaria at Jacob's well,

"The woman said to him, 'I know that Messiah is coming (he who is called Christ). When he comes, he will tell us all things.' Jesus said to her, 'I who speak to you am he.'" John 4:25-26 (ESV)

There is also a story in Matthew 16 where Jesus asks the disciples who the people think is the Son of Man. They say that some believe it is John the Baptist, and they mention others. Jesus asked them,

"'But who do you say that I am?' Simon Peter said in reply, 'You are the Messiah, the Son of the living God.'" Matt 16:16 (NABRE)

Jesus is pleased that God has revealed that to Peter and tells him that he is the rock upon which he will build his church.

There is a lot of discussion in the gospels about Jesus performing miracles. Scholars generally believe that descriptions of some of these miracles are included to show that Jesus was the Messiah and the Son of God. Some examples are: he cleanses a Leper who asks to be made clean and heals a Centurion's Servant. The centurion believes that Jesus can cure illness, and Jesus rewards him for that faith by curing his servant. He cures Peter's mother-in-law of a fever, presumably to lessen the burden on Peter's wife, as Peter follows Jesus. When word got around, people brought others who were sick or possessed by demons, and Matthew 8:16 says that Jesus cured them all. In another instance, he calms a storm at sea, and even his disciples were amazed that he could command the winds and the sea. He walks on water. He feeds thousands of people by multiplying a few loaves of bread and fish.

People heard about the amazing things that Jesus was doing, and when he was at the temple in Jerusalem, they confronted him,

"So the Jews gathered around him and said to him, 'How long are you going to keep us in suspense? If you are the Messiah, tell us plainly.' Jesus answered them, 'I told you and you do not believe. The works I do in my Father's name testify to me. But you do not believe,..." John 10:24-26 (NABRE)

This makes it clear that Jesus claimed he was the Messiah and that the miracles were supposed to demonstrate that to the people. He tells them that the people who believe in him are given eternal life and reinforces that he is the son of God,

"The Father and I are one." John 10:30 (NABRE)

It also shows that even in the face of miracles, some do not believe. The people pick up rocks to stone him, and Jesus says,

"I have shown you many good works from my Father. For which of these are you trying to stone me?" The Jews answered him, "We are not stoning you for a good work but for blasphemy. You, a man, are making yourself God." John 10:32-33 (NABRE)

Jesus escaped, but these teachings show that Jesus did claim to be the Messiah and the Son of God, but some Jews were unwilling to accept that even in the face of his performing miracles to prove it to them.

As described in John 11, Jesus continues performing miracles and brings a man named Lazarus back to life, who had been dead for four days. Thus demonstrating his power over life and death. This made many people believe in him, but some went and told the Pharisees. The Pharisees get upset and fear that everybody will believe in Jesus after that miracle, and that will cause problems for them with the Romans. They fear they will lose their power and position, and they begin to plot against him.

Jesus continued preaching and performing miracles. He raised a girl who had just died from the dead, he cured two blind men, a woman who had great faith in him was cured by just touching the hem of his garment, and he healed a mute person.

There is an event at the Feast of Tabernacle that I will discuss in the section on Jesus' death and resurrection; however, at one point, the people at the temple, impressed with his teachings, are again asking who he is.

"So Jesus told them, "When you have lifted up the Son of Man, then you will know that I AM, and that I do

nothing on my own authority. Instead, I speak only what the Father has taught me." John 8:28 (ESV)

Jesus is declaring himself to be the Son of Man and is using the same words that God said to Moses,

"God said to Moses, 'I AM who I AM.' And he said, 'Say this to the people of Israel: 'I AM has sent me to you.'" Exod 3:14 (ESV)

It is clear that Jesus did claim to be the Messiah and the Son of God, and he performed a variety of miracles, including raising people from the dead to prove it. This caused some people to believe in him and caused the powerful elite in the Jewish faith to fear him.

I will discuss Jesus' trial and crucifixion in another section, but in that trial, Jesus confirmed who he was,

"Again the high priest asked him and said to him, 'Are you the Messiah, the son of the Blessed One?' Then Jesus answered, 'I am'" Mark 14:61-62. (NABRE)

Destruction of the Temple and the End of Days

Summary

- Jesus foretold the temple's destruction and many related events, which happened later, in 70 AD.
- Only God knows when the end of days will happen.
- We should not worry about it. Instead, we should live our lives, do God's will as Jesus has taught us, and we will be saved in the end.

Discussion

Chapter 24 of Matthew discusses Jesus' prediction that the temple will be destroyed and discusses the end of days. The disciples ask Jesus when it will happen, and he says it will be in their generation. He mentions that there will be false messiahs, wars, earthquakes, and other dreadful things that will happen and that the disciples will be persecuted, but if they preserve, they will be saved. He mentions that when this all happens, the Jews must flee to the mountains. All of that occurred in 70 AD; there were wars, the Jews revolted against Rome, and, as you would expect, they killed many Jews and destroyed the temple. Some of the disciples were persecuted and killed before and after that happened.

The disciples may have thought that the end of days is related to the temple's destruction, but Jesus does not say that. He says that the things he mentioned will be just the beginning of the labor pains. Before his coming again, the skies will darken, and then a sign of the Son of Man will appear in the skies. He will be seen coming upon the clouds. Angels will sound trumpet blasts and will gather all the faithful. He mentions that the faithful will disappear, and the others will be left. This is probably the origin of rapture stories.

He makes it clear that many dreadful things may happen before the end of days, but we should use our God-given talents and even develop more talents in service of God. We should always be ready and in good standing with God. Only God knows when the end of days will happen. He assures us that, in the end, the righteous will go with God to eternal life, and everyone else will go to eternal punishment.

If you are interested in the details, please read them in the Bible. It is all pretty vague, and people have thought several times in the past that all the signs have happened and the end was near. Yet here we are 1,990 years later, and it has not occurred yet.

The main actionable message I took out of these chapters is that we cannot know when the end of days will happen. We should not worry about it. Instead, we should live our lives, use the talents God gave us, improve on them, continue to seek God, keep our faith, and do God's will, and we will be saved in the end.

Miscellaneous Topics

Several other miscellaneous topics are often discussed related to Jesus and his teachings or the practices of the church in relation to his teachings. I address some of those in this section.

Fornication and Homosexuality

Judging by how much discussion I see about these topics in the media and religious forums, this is an area of keen interest. People who participate in sex outside of marriage (fornication) and people who have same-sex relations (homosexuality) want those behaviors legitimized by their churches. They are applying significant pressure in their various denominations. Many people assert that Jesus had nothing to say about either topic. However, I did not find that to be true.

Summary

- The Old Testament view was that any sexual activity outside of marriage is wrong.
- Jesus did not modify this view. Jesus taught that sexual immorality (*porneia*) was a sin, and that included fornication (sex outside of marriage) and homosexual and lesbian behavior.
- Jesus said that marriage is defined as being between a man and a woman, which means that God does not condone same-sex marriage.
- The practice of male homosexual behavior is specifically condemned in both the Old Testament and the New Testament.
- Female lesbian relationships are not directly discussed; there is just one direct reference to them being "unnatural."

Discussion

Many people assert that Jesus does not talk specifically about fornication (sex outside the context of marriage) or homosexual relations. That is not true; Jesus does condemn sexual immorality in multiple places. To understand what constituted sexual immorality in Jesus' day, I had to do some research.

First, Jesus likely did not think he needed need to list every type of sexual behavior and call them out separately since it is addressed in the Old Testament. Deuteronomy 22:28-29 makes it clear that if a man has sex with an unmarried virgin woman, he must marry her. If she is not a virgin, then she is another man's wife, so it is adultery. Deuteronomy 22:13–21 makes it clear that if a woman is found not to be a virgin on her wedding night, she should be stoned to death because she has committed a disgraceful act.

The implications are clear in the Old Testament that sexual activity outside of marriage is a sin, and the man and woman involved must marry. If they have sex with anyone else after that point, it is adultery. If they do not marry, it could end up causing the death of the woman. Fortunately, Jesus ended the stoning practice by making it clear that he who is without sin should cast the first stone, which is nobody, John 8:7-11. But he did not change the definition of sin.

In the Old Testament, Leviticus is quite clear about the topic of male homosexual practices. In discussing the laws related to sexual behavior. It says,

"You shall not lie with a male as with a woman; it is an abomination." Lev 18:22 (ESV)

"If a man lies with a male as with a woman, both of them have committed an abomination; they shall surely be put to death; their blood is upon them." Lev 20:13 (ESV)

These passages are the most direct in condemning male homosexual behavior. The definition of *"lie with a male as with a woman"* is a broad statement of condemnation of male with male sexual behavior. Leviticus is silent on lesbian sexual behavior.

The Old Testament is in the Christian bible because it still applies unless Jesus modified some teaching or another. However, some people do not like to accept Old Testament teachings, so let us examine what Jesus said,

"For out of the heart come evil thoughts, murder, adultery, sexual immorality, theft, false witness, slander. These are what defile a person." Matt 15:19-20 (ESV)

"For from within, out of the heart of man, come evil thoughts, sexual immorality, theft, murder, adultery, coveting, wickedness, deceit, sensuality, envy, slander, pride, foolishness. All these evil things come from within, and they defile a person." Mark 7:21-23 (ESV)

To understand this statement, we need to understand what the terms Jesus used meant. The original word used in the earliest Greek that has been translated to *"sexual immorality"* was *"porneia."* I spent some time researching that word. Greek Lexicons provide definitions of the ancient Greek words used in the New Testament. According to Strong's G4202 Greek Lexicon, *"porneia,"* at the time of Jesus, meant any form of illicit sexual intercourse, which included prostitution, adultery, pedophilia, homosexuality, lesbianism, incest, fornication, and bestiality. I looked at other lexicons and theological dictionaries as well. Some have the same definition, and some just say, "any sexual relations outside of marriage." Some say "illicit sexual relations of any kind" or "unlawful sexual intercourse," but those are not especially useful since they do not define illicit or unlawful behaviors. I looked to see what New Testament scholars and linguistic experts say, and almost all of them conclude that all sexual relations outside of marriage are included in the meaning of "*porneia*" at the time of Jesus.

So, Jesus' statement indicates that any sexual relations between unmarried people defiles a person along with all the other behaviors listed. Sex between an unmarried person and a married person is Adultery, so that is covered. Any kind of group sex would include behaviors from this list. Marriage is clearly defined in the Old and New Testaments as between a man and a woman (see the section about marriage.) All that is left that does not defile a person is sex between a man and a woman who are husband and wife.

The word "*porneia*" is used in 26 places in the original Greek New Testament by Jesus and the disciples; let us examine a few of them. In Paul's letter to the Galatians, one of the earliest books written,

"Now the works of the flesh are evident: sexual immorality (porneia), impurity, sensuality, idolatry, sorcery, enmity, strife, jealousy, fits of anger, rivalries, dissensions, divisions, envy, drunkenness, orgies, and things like these. I warn you, as I warned you before, that those who do such things will not inherit the kingdom of God." Gal 5:19-21 (ESV)

This summarizes several of Jesus' teachings and supports his teachings on immoral behavior. Paul, in his first letter to the Corinthians, discusses this topic,

"Flee from sexual immorality (porneia). Every other sin a person commits is outside the body, but the sexually immoral person sins against his own body." 1 Cor 6:18 (ESV)

Paul is echoing Jesus' teaching and is saying that we should avoid all the sexually immoral behavior that is implied by the term porneia.

"'It is good for a man not to have sexual relations with a woman.' But because of the temptation to sexual immorality (porneia), each man should have his own wife and each woman her own husband. The husband should give to his wife her conjugal rights, and likewise the wife to her husband." 1 Cor 7:1-3 (ESV)

"To the unmarried and the widows I say that it is good for them to remain single, as I am. But if they cannot exercise self-control, they should marry. For it is better to marry than to burn with passion." Cor 7:8-9 (ESV)

Paul is saying that sex outside of marriage is immoral, and if you desire to have sex and cannot control yourself, you should marry.

Corinthians, in the New Testament, addresses the topic of male homosexuality as follows:

"Do you not know that the unjust will not inherit the kingdom of God? Do not be deceived; neither fornicators nor idolaters nor adulterers nor boy prostitutes nor sodomites [nor men who practice homosexuality]." 1 Cor 6:9 (NABRE)

Note that some translations use *"males who have sex with males"* or a variation of that and avoid the terms *"sodomite"* or *"homosexual"* that are used in NABRE and ESV. Some people claim that all these are mistranslations; however, after reading many discussions about the original Greek, *"men who lie with a male"* is a well-supported translation and agrees with the clear wording in Leviticus shown above.

Paul's letter to the Romans addresses the topic of homosexuality as follows as part of a discussion about Jesus' teachings about various sins. It is the only place I found that mentions female homosexuality directly,

"Therefore, God handed them over to degrading passions. Their females exchanged natural relations for unnatural, and the males likewise gave up natural relations with females and burned with lust for one another. Males did shameful things with males and thus received in their own persons the due penalty for their perversity." Rom 1:26-27 (NABRE)

The teachings discussed above support the assertion that Jesus viewed homosexuality as unnatural.

I could not find any teachings of Jesus that would imply that when he discussed sexual immorality, *"porneia,"* it excluded sex outside of marriage or homosexual behavior.

The assertion of some is that Jesus did not intend to imply that sex outside of marriage or homosexual and lesbian activity is illicit. Others point out that he would have phrased it differently or listed the subset of sins that he intended if he meant to exclude them. I also found no teachings that changed the Old Testament rules on these subjects.

In summary, the inescapable conclusion is that Jesus viewed all sexual relations outside of marriage as sin and that only marriage between a man and a woman is condoned by God. I know this is not what people want to hear, but that conclusion is well-supported by reading the scriptures.

Some churches have decided that Jesus and his disciples did not understand the concept of sexual orientation and did not consider the possibility of committed, monogamous same sex relationships. They assert that if they did, they would have condoned them, and some churches now condone same-sex marriage. I could not find support for that view in the Bible.

These teachings do not mean that people who have engaged in sexual relations outside of marriage, or committed adultery, homosexual sex, and all the other behaviors mentioned above should be excluded from the church or that they cannot be saved and go to heaven. These teachings indicate that these behaviors are sins. We are expected to refrain from sin, repent, ask forgiveness when we do sin, and try to stop committing the sin. If we continue committing the sin, it is evidence that we did not repent.

A House Divided

After Jesus cast a demon out of a man, some Pharisees or Scribes said to the people that Jesus must be in league with the devil to be able to do that. Jesus tells them that it is silly by saying,

"How can Satan cast out Satan? If a kingdom is divided against itself, that kingdom cannot stand. And if a house is divided against itself, that house will not be able to stand. And if Satan has risen up against himself and is divided, he cannot stand, but is coming to an end." Mark 2:23-26 (ESV)

This passage or a similar version in Matthew is the origin of the phrase, "A house divided against itself cannot stand," which was said by Abraham Lincoln.

Pay your Taxes and Give to the Church

Amazingly, Jesus did address paying your taxes as well as giving to God and the church.

Summary

- Pay your taxes to avoid getting into trouble.
- Give God what he is due: your faith, love, and obedience.
- Give to your church what your heart says to give.

Discussion

There is a story in Matthew 17 about when Jesus went to Capernaum, and the temple tax collector asked about Jesus paying his temple tax. Every Jew had to pay half a shekel a year to support the temple. Jesus points out that the temple belongs to the lord, and he is the lord, so he should be exempt. However, since most people did not accept that, he instructed Peter to go catch a fish and told him that he would find a coin in the mouth of the fish and he should use it to pay the tax for himself and Jesus to avoid offending and causing issues, Matt 17:24-27.

There is another story in Matthew 22 where the Pharisees try to trap Jesus again. They sent somebody to ask him if it was lawful to pay the Roman taxes. They hoped he would say no, which would turn the Romans against him. Jesus says,

"'Show me the coin for the tax.' And they brought him a denarius. And Jesus said to them, 'Whose likeness and inscription is this?' They said, 'Caesar's.' Then he said to them, 'Therefore render to Caesar the things that are Caesar's, and to God the things that are God's.'" Matt 22:19-21 (ESV)

It is good advice to pay your taxes to the church and the government so they do not punish you. Some suggest that it could also imply rebellion against Rome instead if that is what Rome is due. But you should also give to God what is his, which is your faith and obedience. Some people use this passage to say you should give an equal amount of money to the church, but it does not seem to say that. What does God care about money?

The idea of paying a tithe of 10% to the church comes from Leviticus 27:30. But Jesus indirectly addresses that in another teaching. While he is denouncing the scribes and the Pharisees, he says,

"Woe to you, scribes and Pharisees, hypocrites! For you tithe mint and dill and cumin, and have neglected the weightier matters of the law: justice and mercy and faithfulness. These you ought to have done, without neglecting the others." Matt 23:23 (ESV)

So, he is admonishing them for paying their tithe but ignoring matters of God's laws and faith. Many suggest that Jesus suggests they should pay attention to both God's laws and faith and tithe if that is their custom. Others think that it implies that Jesus is saying to tithe. Jesus does not address that issue otherwise. However, it is addressed elsewhere in the New Testament,

"The point is this: whoever sows sparingly will also reap sparingly, and whoever sows bountifully will also reap bountifully. Each one must give as he has decided in his heart, not reluctantly or under compulsion, for God loves a cheerful giver." 2 Cor 9:6-7 (ESV)

This teaching implies that we should give what our heart says to give; we are not under compulsion to give a specific amount.

Jesus and the Rules in Leviticus

Summary

- The rules related to the Priests of Levi and the Jewish civil and ceremonial practices no longer apply.
- Food laws, rules about executing people for many sins, performing ritual animal sacrifices, restrictions about the Sabbath, fasting, and many others no longer apply; see the discussion.
- We are still supposed to avoid meat that was used in pagan sacrifices, drain blood from and cook meat.
- The moral rules in Leviticus 18 and some of the rules of conduct in Leviticus 19 still apply.

Discussion

There are some rules in Leviticus that no longer apply because Jesus changed them. Some assert that the whole thing no longer applies, but I do not see support for that in Jesus' teachings. Jesus said,

"Do not think that I have come to abolish the law or the prophets. I have come not to abolish but to fulfill. Amen, I say to you, until heaven and earth pass away, not the smallest letter or the smallest part of a letter will pass from the law, until all things have taken place." Matt 5:17-18 (NABRE)

Jesus affirms in the Sermon on the Mount that the old rules still apply, but then he proceeds to change some of them. That leaves us to conclude that they apply except where he specifically modifies them. Much of Leviticus deals with priests from the tribe of Levi and all the rituals and traditions for Jewish religious practice. There are also rules related to civic issues like the sale of property, slavery, and economic issues. Then, there are moral, behavioral, and ethical rules. Some of these rules do not apply anymore, some have been modified, and some still apply unchanged today.

One area that people often ask about is dietary restrictions. Mark says that Jesus changed that when Jesus said,

"'Do you not see that whatever goes into a person from outside cannot defile him, since it enters not his heart but his stomach, and is expelled?' (Thus he declared all foods clean.)" Mark 7:18-19 (ESV)

This is also addressed in Acts 10:9-16. Jesus addressed the practice of stoning people to death for various sins when he said,

"Let him who is without sin among you be the first to throw a stone" John 8:7 (ESV)

No one is without sin, so no one should cast a stone. Jesus asserted that following traditions and performing ceremonies was less important than following God's commandments. He addresses this in multiple places in the Bible, usually where he criticizes the Pharisees, as discussed in prior sections.

The question about the other rules in Leviticus is addressed in Acts 15, which was written by Luke. Someone was teaching the Gentiles without permission about things related to Leviticus, like circumcision, and was upsetting them. Paul, Barnabas, and some others are sent to talk to the apostles and elders of the Council of Jerusalem about this topic (around 50 AD). The apostles, including Peter and James, the brother of Jesus, and other elders, debated the issue. They decide to send a couple of people to the Gentiles to clarify what applies along with a letter. It says,

"For it has seemed good to the Holy Spirit and to us to lay on you no greater burden than these require-ments: that you abstain from what has been sacrificed to idols, and from blood, and from what has been strangled, and from sexual immorality. If you keep yourselves from these, you will do well." Acts 15:28-29 (ESV).

This is taken to mean that the coming of the Messiah has changed things. People do not need to become Jews and follow the Jewish governmental and ceremonial rules and traditions to follow Jesus. We are still supposed to avoid meat that has been offered in pagan sacrifices, and we should still drain the blood and cook the meat, but otherwise, all meat is fine. Most of the civil and ceremonial rules in Leviticus no longer apply, with the exceptions noted. However, the moral laws do still apply today, and Jesus himself confirmed that, as discussed in prior sections. This got rid of the rules about executing people for many sins, performing ritual animal sacrifices, restrictions about the Sabbath, fasting, burnt offerings, food rules, isolation of women during menses, circumcision requirements, rules about how we cut our hair, wearing of mixed fabrics, purification rituals, etc. and the various Jewish ceremonial practices.

In general, the moral rules in Leviticus 18 still apply, and they are reinforced in many places in the New Testament, for example, Matt 15:19-20, Mark 7:21-23, Acts 15:20, 15:29, 21:25, Rom 1:26-27, 13:13, 1 Cor 5:1, 6:9-10, and other places. Those who assert that these rules no longer apply appear to ignore the ample evidence in the New Testament confirming that they do still apply.

Many of the rules of conduct in Leviticus 19 still apply and are reinforced in the New Testament, like the rules that mirror the commandments. However, some of those rules relate more to ceremonial practices and the consensus of scholars is that they no longer apply.

What About Tattoos?

Summary

- The Leviticus statement about tattoos probably no longer applies per Acts 15:28-29.
- Choose tattoos that do not defile you in God's eyes.

Discussion

Leviticus says,

"You shall not make any cuts on your body for the dead or tattoo yourselves" Lev 19:28 (ESV)

Some current-day churches interpret this to mean that tattoos of all types are forbidden. There is some debate about if this rule still applies. Most agree that the rule about making cuts on your body for the dead was related to pagan practices of mourning. The original word used was not tattoos; it was marks. It is also unclear if the marks referred to are marks for the dead or marks in general. The rules in the same section about how we cut our hair and beards are thought to no longer apply. Most people think that this rule, if it still applies, does not relate to today's decorative tattoos. Based on the statement in Acts 15:28-29 discussed in the previous section, it appears that this rule no longer applies.

Some people suggest that we consider these passages before we decide what tattoos to get,

"Or do you not know that your body is a temple of the Holy Spirit within you, whom you have from God? You are not your own, for you were bought with a price. So glorify God in your body." 1 Cor 6:19-20 (ESV)

"I appeal to you therefore, brothers, by the mercies of God, to present your bodies as a living sacrifice, holy and acceptable to God, which is your spiritual worship."
Rom 12:1 (ESV)

So perhaps we should avoid tattoos that would defile our bodies in the eyes of God, like pagan or satanic symbols or other signs associated with evil.

Drinking Alcohol

The Old Testament says that wine is a gift from God to gladden the heart of man (Psalm 104:14–15) and to drink wine with a merry or joyful heart (Ecclesiastes 9:7) but speaks against drunkenness (for example, 1 Samuel 1:14, Tobit 4:15, Proverbs 20:1, Proverbs 23:20, Isaiah 5:11-12). There was a very practical reason why people drank beer and wine at that time. Drinking water was not always safe because of bacteria, but the process of fermenting beer, wine, and other spirits kills bacteria. So, drinking beer and wine was safer and was a common practice. It is assumed that the alcohol content was lower than today's beer and wine, so it took a lot to get drunk.

Jesus did not directly address drinking in his teachings. However, Jesus himself is described as drinking wine in the Bible (Matt 11:19, Matt 26:29, Mark 14:25, Mark 15:36, Luke 7:34, Luke 22:18, John 19:30). The first miracle that Jesus performed, that his disciples observed, was turning water into wine at a wedding in Cana that he attended (John 2:1-11). If Jesus did not approve of drinking wine, he probably would not have done that. Jesus also said that nothing we consume defiles us (Mark 7:15, 7:18-20). So, it is apparent that Jesus was fine with people drinking. In the New Testament, Ephesians 5:18 and Galatians 5:21 reinforce the Old Testament teaching not to get drunk.

Abortion

Neither the Old Testament nor the New Testament addresses abortion. There is a rule mentioned in the Old Testament addressing the penalty for accidentally causing a woman to miscarry, but that is it. There are several passages in the bible that people use to support the thought that God sees fetuses as people in the womb. Other passages are cited that support the notion that the spirit enters the body when the baby takes its first breath. We know from science that life begins at conception. However, there are no scriptures that tell us when the soul enters the fetus to guide us on the morality of abortion. However, there are works of the Apostolic Fathers like the *Didache* and the *Epistle of Barnabas* that say, *"you shall not abort a child or commit infanticide"* Holmes. *The Apostolic Fathers in English* (p. 239 and similar words p. 291). Clement of Alexandria and others also specifically condemn abortion. While these writings were not chosen to be in the Bible, they are an important part of early Christian teachings.

The largest Christian denomination in the world, the Catholic Church, and the second largest, the Eastern Orthodox Church, assert that the soul enters the body at conception, and they see abortion as murder and is thus prohibited. However, there are some narrowly defined exceptions related to care required to save the mother's life that could end the pregnancy. Some protestant denominations have a very similar view to the Catholic Church.

Other churches allow for exceptions early in the pregnancy, in addition to exceptions when abortion is needed to save the life of the mother. This stance is possibly based on Thomas Aquinas' (1225-1274 AD) assertion that the soul did not enter the fetus until around forty days after conception. Some churches draw the line at the point when the fetus is viable. Most churches condemn abortion for birth control or gender selection. However, some Christian denominations do not condemn abortion at any time and leave the choice to the woman. The Christian world has not come to a consensus on this topic. The lack of specific guidance on this issue in the Bible has caused that situation.

Attending Mass or Church

Summary

- Going to church can be a terrific way to keep the Sabbath holy, but neither God nor Jesus instructs that we must attend church.

Discussion

Some churches assert that you must attend mass or church. Some even say it is a serious sin not to attend. The Bible passage most often quoted in relation to this question is one of the commandments,

"Remember the Sabbath day, to keep it holy. Six days you shall labor, and do all your work, but the seventh day is a Sabbath to the Lord *your God. On it you shall not do any work, ..."* Exod 20:8-11 (ESV)

There are three clear specifics here: remember the Sabbath day, keep it holy, and abstain from work in order that you might rest. There are no specifics about what keeping it holy means or what work we must refrain from. In Jesus' day, the Jews had taken the not working part way too far such that you could not even prepare food, light a fire, write, wash, walk over a certain distance, and many other things. That is why Jesus told the Pharisees that they were missing the point and that they had made the Sabbath a burden; Jesus said,

"The sabbath was made for man, not man for the sabbath." Mark 2:27 (ESV)

Jesus made it clear that any onerous rules or traditions around the Sabbath no longer apply. Some scholars suggest that Jesus thought we should rest from our servile labor, and it is okay if we do minor labor required for living life. Others suggest that working to perform an act of charity is acceptable. Others believe he lifted the prohibition to work. However, the commands remain to remember the Sabbath and keep it holy.

Jesus simply did not say that we must attend church. The Old Testament does not ever mention synagogues. Jesus did attend synagogue at times during his ministry, but he does not say that we must do so. There are a few statements in Acts and in some of the letters of Paul that encourage going to church, but even there, I could not find any commands that we must do so. This statement in Hebrews is often quoted,

"And let us consider how to stir up one another to love and good works, not neglecting to meet together, as is the habit of some, but encouraging one another, and all the more as you see the Day drawing near." Heb 10:24-25 (ESV)

This is the closest thing to a statement in the Bible that we should attend church, but it is not a command to do so. The origins of Hebrews are questioned, even by the Catholic Church. It was not likely written by Paul. Many scholars think that it reflects the teachings of the early church.

Some churches quote a saying by Jesus as support that we should attend church,

"For where two or three are gathered in my name, there am I among them." Matt 18:20 (ESV)

In context, this statement is in the teaching about what to do if your brother sins against you. If you cannot work it out directly with him, you are supposed to gather one or two witnesses and try again. So, this passage has nothing to do with church attendance.

There can be value in attending church in reinforcing your faith. Hearing the messages delivered in the service and the fellowship of other Christians can bolster your faith. However, you need to find a church that does that.

I once attended a service at a big church in my town with a friend. I was excited; it was much bigger than my church, and there were many people there. When the service started, my feelings quickly changed. Almost the whole service was dedicated to telling us why we needed to dig deep in our pockets and give our money to the church to build a new building. I do not remember anything about God or Jesus from that service. I never went back, and it might be the origin of some skepticism about organized religion. I have also attended some really moving services at other churches. The people were friendly in most of the services I attended, but often, it felt like everybody was just going through the motions. In the right church, it seems like a terrific way to keep the Sabbath holy, not so much otherwise.

So, I conclude that attending church can be a terrific way to keep the Sabbath holy, but neither God nor Jesus instructs us to attend church. They leave it to each of us to decide how to keep it holy.

The Role of Women in the Church

Summary

- Jesus treated men and women equally even though the dominant culture at the time did not.
- There are no direct teachings of Jesus about the roles of men and women in the church.

Discussion

The role of women in Christian teaching varies by denomination. The Catholic church prohibits women from being deacons, priests, bishops, cardinals, or the pope. Their view is that women cannot receive the sacrament of holy orders. Some protestant churches allow women in ordained clergy roles, and others do not.

There are a few bible passages quoted to support the Catholic view. When I looked for information about why the Catholic church has this view, I see them often cite,

"As in all the churches of the saints, the women should keep silent in the churches. For they are not permitted to speak, but should be in submission, as the Law also says. If there is anything they desire to learn, let them ask their husbands at home. For it is shameful for a woman to speak in church." 1 Cor 14:32-37 (ESV)

That certainly tells us Paul's view on the matter or that of the early church. However, the focus of this book is the teaching of Jesus. Throughout the Gospels, Jesus held women in high regard, and he talked to them in public, which was against tradition at the time, answered their questions, and performed healing miracles for them just like for men. Luke tells us that in addition to the twelve disciples, several women were followers of Jesus,

"Soon afterward he went on through cities and villages, proclaiming and bringing the good news of the kingdom of God. And the twelve were with him, and also some women who had been healed of evil spirits and infirmities: Mary, called Magdalene, from whom seven demons had gone out, and Joanna, the wife of Chuza, Herod's household manager, and Susanna, and many others, who provided for them out of their means." Luke 8:1-3 (ESV)

Are these women disciples of Jesus in the same sense as the twelve? Some people think so. When Jesus sent out his twelve disciples two-by-two to spread his teachings (Luke 9:1-6), it only mentions him sending the twelve men. When Jesus sends out seventy-two of his followers (Luke 10:1-12) to teach, it does not say if they are just men. Perhaps Jesus did not send out his female disciples because he knew it was too dangerous for them.

I could not find any times in the Bible when Jesus says anything to imply that women are not equal in his eyes or any actions of his that imply that to be the case. He taught to women as well as men. He ended the practice of men being able to just dismiss their wives. He ended the practice of stoning women for committing adultery. The first time he directly declared that he was the Messiah was to a Samarian woman. The Gospels also tell us that Jesus appeared first to Mary Magdalene after the resurrection, and he sent her to spread the word to the other disciples.

So, by his actions, Jesus showed that women were equal. The dominant culture at the time of Jesus discriminated against women and relegated them to certain roles, but we do not see Jesus doing that. It is unclear what the basis of Paul's statement is in Corinthians. I do not see any teachings of Jesus that support that stance. The Old Testament stance on women is mixed. Sometimes, they are described as under the control of men like their fathers or husbands. But there are also women in leadership roles in places in the Old Testament, and even a female prophet, Huldah, mentioned in 2 Kings 22. This passage certainly implies that men and women are equal in Jesus' eyes,

"There is neither Jew nor Greek, there is neither slave nor free, there is no male and female, for you are all one in Christ Jesus." Gal 3:28(ESV)

Jesus did not teach directly on this topic that we know of. John mentions that Jesus did and presumably taught many other things that are not in the Gospels (John 21:25). Perhaps the men who wrote the Gospels did not choose to pass on any teachings about the role of women. However, based on his actions, Jesus viewed men and women as equals.

Celibacy of Priests or Ministers

As quoted earlier, Jesus acknowledges that some people *"become eunuchs"* for the kingdom of God in Matthew 19:12. In that teaching, he neither encourages nor discourages that practice. No other teachings of Jesus address whether church leaders of any type must remain celibate. It was also not a Jewish practice in Jesus' time for church leaders to stay unmarried or celibate except in one situation. High priests were expected to abstain from intercourse with their wives when they served in the temple (temple service was a rotating duty).

There are related discussions on this subject in Paul's letters. One mentions that unmarried men are less distracted with worldly affairs, but he does not say that church leaders must not marry (1 Corinthians 7:32-34). So, at most, Paul may be encouraging the idea but not mandating it. Other passages in later letters discuss how church leaders should manage their families and children well, seeming to assume that they will be married.

The practice of celibacy of priests or ministers is a church tradition or a mandated practice. However, I found nothing in the Bible that mandates that tradition or practice. In fact, Peter, viewed by the Catholic Church as the first Pope was married (see the mention of Jesus curing his mother-in-law of fever in Matthew 8:14-15, Mark 1:29-31, and Luke 4:38.)

What do we know about Mary Magdalene?

Summary

- Jesus drove seven demons out of her.
- She followed Jesus starting when he was in Galilee.
- She may be from the town of Magdala.
- She was there at the crucifixion and resurrection.
- There is nothing in the Bible to indicate that she was a prostitute or that she and Jesus had a relationship beyond that of teacher and student.

Discussion

We do not know much other than she was a follower of Jesus. There are no discussions between her and Jesus mentioned in the bible. There is no hint of a relationship between her and Jesus. The common belief of many is that Mary Magdalene was a prostitute redeemed by Jesus. However, the Bible never says or even implies that to be the case. Luke and Mark say,

"And the twelve were with him, and also some women who had been healed of evil spirits and infirmities: Mary, called Magdalene, from whom seven demons had gone out, and..." Luke 8:1-3 (ESV)

"Now when he rose early on the first day of the week, he appeared first to Mary Magdalene, from whom he had cast out seven demons." Mark 16:9 (ESV)

So, from these passages, we can assume that Jesus cast seven demons out of Mary and that she became his follower. Also, that Jesus appeared to her first when he was resurrected. All the other references to her are related to her presence at the crucifixion and when Jesus was resurrected. In Mark, it says:

"There were also women looking on from a distance, among whom were Mary Magdalene, and Mary the mother of James the younger and of Joses, and Salome. When he was in Galilee, they followed him and ministered to him, and there were also many other women who came up with him to Jerusalem." Mark 15:40-41 (ESV)

From this, we can infer that she had followed him in Galilee. We do not know when she and Jesus met, when he cast out the demons, or what she did before that. Magdala was a fishing town on the west coast of the Sea of Galilee, so it is assumed that she is from there.

The portrayal of Mary Magdalene as a prostitute came from Pope Gregory 1 in 591, conflating her with "a sinful woman," who is not named but who anointed Jesus' feet in Luke 7:36-50. Nothing in those passages indicates that the woman is Mary Magdalene. Pope Paul VI corrected this in 1969, but it is hard to combat hundreds of years of misinformation.

There is no mention of her after the resurrection. She is not mentioned in Acts or any of the letters. The Gospel of Mary is dated to a later period, so she did not likely write it. There are mentions of her in other later writings of questionable origin, but none of them are viewed as authentic. Eastern tradition is that she went with the disciple John to Ephesus and later died there. There is another story that she went to France and lived out her life there. Both of those appear to be unsupported by any historical evidence.

What Places Did Jesus Visit?

Most of the events mentioned in the New Testament were in areas of Galilee and Judea, but Jesus is mentioned in the Gospels as visiting places in Samaria, Perea, Decapolis, Gaulanitis, and Phoenicia. Primarily all around the Sea of Galilee, east and west of the Jordan River, and south to the area of Jerusalem. Today, these areas are in Israel, the West Bank, western Jordan, western Syria, and southern Lebanon.

The distance between the place farthest north mentioned and the place farthest south mentioned is about one hundred miles, but with the mountain ranges in that area, the walking distance would be longer. People have analyzed the Gospels, taken note of the places Jesus visited in the order mentioned, and tried to calculate how much Jesus and the disciples walked.

Some calculate numbers over 3,000 thousand miles (see blessitt.com/miles-jesus-and-mary-walked). That seems like a lot, but even if it is 3,000 miles, assuming a three-year ministry, that averages about nineteen miles per week. They could likely walk nineteen miles or more in a day. Looking at it that way, that number is possible.

Chapter 3: The Death and Resurrection of Jesus

The gospels extensively discuss the events leading up to Jesus being crucified and his resurrection. That topic alone can and does fill books on its own. That part of Jesus' story is not the focus of this book. However, I will summarize the events in this section to highlight the specific teachings of Jesus, which are considered central to Christianity, from this time in his life.

Jesus Angers the Pharisees

Jesus' problems with the Jewish leadership began early in his ministry. The Pharisees and Sadducees were already aware of John the Baptist and were watching him. When some of them came to see what he was doing in baptizing people, he taunted them and called them a brood of vipers (Matthew 2:7).

As Jesus taught and performed miracles, various Scribes and Pharisees noticed. They did not like that Jesus was seen with sinners and tax collectors (Matt 8:11). When they learned of him casting out demons and doing healing, like healing a mute person and some blind men and restoring a recently deceased girl back to life, they claimed that he did so by the prince of demons, not by God. (Matt 9:34). When the Pharisees saw Jesus' disciples picking and eating grain on the Sabbath, they were upset. They accused the disciples of breaking the law by doing work on the Sabbath. Jesus pointed out that the Pharisees are allowed to work on the Sabbath, and so should his disciples, thus equating them to the Pharisees. Jesus continues to question them about what is allowed on the Sabbath and challenges their understanding of the law. He even heals a man with a withered hand in the synagogue, in front of the Pharisees, on the Sabbath.

Matthew and John say,

"But the Pharisees went out and conspired against him, how to destroy him." Matt 12:14 (ESV)

Not all the Pharisees were against Jesus. For example, Nicodemus, a prominent Pharisee, came to talk to Jesus when he was in Jerusalem for the Passover feast. From the account in John 3, Nicodemus seems genuinely interested in learning more about Jesus. And indeed, in John 7:50, Nicodemus defends Jesus to the other Pharisees. However, in multiple passages, it is clear that the other Pharisees do not believe that Jesus is the Messiah, and they feel threatened by his growing popularity. They are also upset by some of his teachings that modify their traditional views.

Jesus Foretells his Demise

Jesus foretold his demise on a few occasions,

"He began to teach them that the Son of Man must suffer greatly and be rejected by the elders, the chief priests, and the scribes, and be killed, and rise after three days." Mark 8:31 (NABRE)

In the story about the Feast of Tabernacles, Jesus knows that people are after him, but during the feast, Jesus goes to the temple and begins to teach. People realize who he is and that some are trying to kill him. He again preaches about doing good works on the Sabbath. The people like his teaching, and the Pharisees hear what is going on and they send guards to arrest him,

Jesus then said, "I will be with you a little longer, and then I am going to him who sent me. You will seek me and you will not find me. Where I am you cannot come." John 7:33-34 (ESV)

However, they did not arrest him, and he continued to teach. Some people were convinced he was the Messiah; even the guards sent to arrest him were amazed by his teaching. They go back to the Pharisees and say so. The Pharisees were upset, and that was when Nicodemus told them to find out what he was doing before they condemned him.

Casting the First Stone

The very next day, the Pharisees brought a woman to the temple who was caught in the act of committing adultery. They assert that the law of Moses commands that they stone her to death. As a test, they ask Jesus what he says about it. Jesus says,

"But when they continued asking him, he straight-ened up and said to them, 'Let the one among you who is without sin be the first to throw a stone at her.'" John 8:7 (NABRE)

The people all drift away, as none of them are without sin until Jesus is alone with the woman. He forgives her and tells her to sin no more. This is one of Jesus' central teachings. It is really a restating of his teaching about judging others from the Sermon on the Mount, but at this moment, he is modifying Old Testament teaching about justice.

Of course, the Pharisees were not happy and challenged Jesus more. He challenges their authority and asserts his authority as coming from God, and he makes it clear that he is the Messiah and the son of God. Some people do not accept that and pick up stones to throw at him, so Jesus leaves. Jesus has made quite a public spectacle and has made it clear who he is, and the Jewish power elite were not happy.

Pharisees Plot Against Jesus

Later, as described in John 11, Jesus brings a man named Lazarus back to life, who had died four days before. When the Pharisees learned of this, they called the Sanhedrin, an assembly of elders who sat as a tribunal. They discuss what to do about Jesus,

"What are we to do? For this man performs many signs. If we let him go on like this, everyone will believe in him, and the Romans will come and take away both our place and our nation." John 11:47-48 (ESV)

They feel threatened by Jesus; they worry that all their people will follow him, and they will lose their position with the Romans.

"So from that day on they made plans to put him to death." John 11:53 (ESV)

Jesus learns about this, leaves the area, and goes to Ephraim, a town northeast of Jerusalem in what is called the West Bank today. He stays there with his disciples for a while, but Passover is coming, and they expect that Jesus will go to Jerusalem for that. Before Passover, Jesus goes to Bethany to see Lazarus, the one he raised from the dead, and has dinner with him. The next day, he heads for Jerusalem for Passover.

The Last Supper

People learn about it and come out to meet him with palm branches. Palm branches historically were used to celebrate victory in King David's time. Jesus also rode into Jerusalem on an ass or donkey, as foretold in prophecy in Zechariah 9:9. The Pharisees are quite upset when they see this.

Washing of the Disciples' Feet

At the Passover dinner, which people call the Last Supper, Jesus washes the feet of his disciples,

"When he had washed their feet and put on his outer garments and resumed his place, he said to them, "Do you understand what I have done to you? You call me Teacher and Lord, and you are right, for so I am. If I then, your Lord and Teacher, have washed your feet, you also ought to wash one another's feet." John 13:12-14 (ESV)

Scholars believe that this is an act of humility and love to provide an example to his disciples. He is telling them that they should act the same. In the early church, some churches did this before communion. Today, some churches still hold this ceremony. The priest, preachers, or bishops wash the feet of the faithful as Jesus did with his disciples. In the Catholic Church, it is frequently done on Holy Thursday, the Thursday before Easter, as part of a reenactment of the Last Supper.

Betrayal of Judas is Foretold

Jesus then announces that one of them will betray him. Peter whispers to him and asks who it is. Jesus tells him it is to the person to whom he gives a morsel that he dips in wine. Jesus hands that morsel to Judas and tells him to "do what you are going to do quickly." The disciples do not know what that means, and they assume Jesus is telling Judas to go buy supplies since he is the keeper of their funds.

Commandment to Love One Another

After Judas leaves, Jesus tells the disciples that he will not be with them much longer, and he says,

"A new commandment I give to you, that you love one another: just as I have loved you, you also are to love one another." John 13:34 (ESV)

This is not a new teaching of Jesus; he taught that you should love your neighbor as yourself and love your enemies previously in his ministry. Here, he reinforces it to the disciples, perhaps to ensure they do not fracture after his death.

After that, still, at the last supper, Peter asks him about his statements that he will be leaving and going where they cannot follow him. He does not understand that Jesus is saying he is going to die and go to heaven. Peter assures him that he will lay down his life for Jesus. Jesus then predicts that Peter will deny him three times. Jesus then reassures them that they have faith in God and in him, and he goes to prepare a place for them.

The First Communion or the New Covenant

In Matthew's and Luke's recounting of the Last Supper, they both describe a ritual performed during the Last Supper that has become central to the Christian faith,

"Now as they were eating, Jesus took bread, and after blessing it broke it and gave it to the disciples, and said, 'Take, eat; this is my body.' And he took a cup, and when he had given thanks he gave it to them, saying, 'Drink of it, all of you, for this is my blood of the covenant, which is poured out for many for the forgiveness of sins. I tell you I will not drink again of this fruit of the vine until that day when I drink it new

with you in my Father's kingdom.'" Matt 26:26-29 (ESV)

This ritual is referred to as Communion. The largest branches of Christianity, which are the Catholic Church and the Eastern Orthodox Church, and others believe that in the process of the blessing (consecration), transubstantiation takes place. The bread becomes Jesus' flesh, and the wine becomes his blood. However, they retain their physical appearance but not the substance of bread and wine. By consuming them, we renew our faith in Jesus, and it nourishes our soul.

Some Protestant churches, like Baptists, see it as sacred but symbolic, and they do it in remembrance of Jesus as he directed. As Jesus did, they bless the bread and the wine or grape juice, and they partake in them in a solemn ceremony of remembrance of Jesus' sacrifice on the cross. In doing so, they renew their faith in Jesus and receive God's grace. They believe that Jesus is present during the process, but not physically or spiritually, in the bread and wine.

There is another view called consubstantiation, held by the Church of England and offshoots like the Methodists. In that view, people believe that when the bread and wine are blessed or consecrated, Jesus' spirit enters the bread and wine, causing them to spiritually become the body and blood of Jesus. Jesus' spirit exists alongside the substance of the bread and wine, which however remain bread and wine.

The Lutheran view is called sacramental union, meaning that the body and blood of Jesus are present in communion, but they do not replace the substance of the bread and wine or imbue the bread and wine with the holy spirit, but rather exist in union with the bread and wine in some way, beyond our understanding.

All four of these views are similar and are all vehemently defended by various Christian communities. Sadly, these different views are a source of schism in Christianity, and people have lost their lives for holding the wrong view.

From my study of Jesus' teachings, it is not clear if Jesus meant that the bread and wine physically became his body and blood, symbolized his body and blood, if the bread and wine were imbued with his spirit in the process, or in some other way his body and blood were in union with the bread and wine. In all four versions of the ritual, the practitioners honor Jesus' instruction to perform the ritual in remembrance of him and his sacrifice for us. I am not sure that it matters which of these views we believe in relation to our salvation.

Whatever you believe about what happens to the bread and wine during communion, during the last supper, Jesus is clearly saying that his blood will be shed for the forgiveness of our sins. Through faith in him, we receive that forgiveness, which is the new covenant. This new covenant replaces the old covenant handed down to Moses, described in the Old Testament, and is a central part of the Christian faith.

Betrayal and Arrest of Jesus

After dinner, they retire to a garden on the Mount of Olives. As predicted, Judas betrayed him for thirty pieces of silver to the high priests, and an armed crowd comes to arrest Jesus. Judas identifies Jesus, and they arrest him. One of the disciples pulls out a sword and cuts off the ear of one of the people arresting Jesus. Jesus tells the disciples,

"Put your sword back into its sheath, for all who take the sword will perish by the sword." Matt 26:52 (NABRE)

This also is a central teaching of Christianity. Some people use this passage to support pacifism, but others point out that Jesus told him to put his sword away, not to throw it away. Clearly, there are valid times to use the sword, just not at that time. Jesus also points out,

"Do you think that I cannot appeal to my Father, and he will at once send me more than twelve legions of angels? But how then should the Scriptures be fulfilled, that it must be so?" Matt 26:53-54 (ESV)

Jesus indicates that he has the power from God to stop what is happening but that it is necessary to fulfill the scriptures. This shows that Jesus willingly submits to what is to come, which is also a central teaching of the Christian faith.

The Trial of Jesus

Jesus is taken to the Jewish high priest, Caiaphas, assembled with the scribes and elders. Peter follows at a distance and slips in with the servants to watch. The accounts in the Gospels vary in the details of what questions were asked, so I will just discuss points of agreement. They bring many witnesses against Jesus, but they are clearly making false claims. Jesus refuses to speak about the testimony of the witnesses, and his answers to the priest's questions just frustrate them. In Mark's account, he says the high priest questioned Jesus one more time,

"'Are you the Messiah, the son of the Blessed One?' Then Jesus answered, 'I am; and you will see the Son of Man seated at the right hand of the Power and coming with the clouds of heaven.'" Mark 14:61-62 (NABRE)

Jesus confirms that he is the Messiah and the Son of God, even though it will result in his death. That was all they needed to hear to condemn Jesus.

During all this, Peter is discovered and confronted about being a follower of Jesus; he is afraid and ends up denying it three times as Jesus foretold. Also, Judas regrets what he did and tries to give back the silver he was paid. The priests do not care and refuse to take it. Judas flings the silver into the temple, goes away, and hangs himself. Matt 27:3-6

They decide Jesus should die, and they take him to Pontius Pilate, the Roman governor, since they did not have the power to execute people. Pilate asked Jesus if he was the king of the Jews. Jesus tells him his kingdom is in heaven, not on earth. Pilate tells the priests he finds no guilt in Jesus and offers to release him. They decline and get the crowd to call for him to die. Pilate, concerned there could be a riot, has Jesus whipped; the guards placed a crown of thorns on his head, put a cloak on him, and sent him out. The priests and guards cry for his crucifixion and convince Pilate to let them crucify Jesus.

Interestingly, all the accounts portray Pilate as being resistant to executing Jesus and placing the blame on the Priests.

The Crucifixion of Jesus

They take Jesus out to the place called Golgotha, where they do crucifixions. One of the gospels says Jesus carries the cross himself; the other three say that a Cyrenian named Simon is forced to carry the cross. It is interesting that the story most repeated is that Jesus carried the cross himself even though Matthew, Mark, and Luke all name Simon as carrying the cross.

So, they crucified Jesus along with two other people. They put a sign saying "King of the Jews" on the cross; they taunt him, and the faithful cry for him, powerless to stop it.

Luke says that at one point Jesus said,

"Father, forgive them, for they know not what they do." Luke 23:34 (ESV)

Luke says that he declared to the other two being crucified beside him,

"Truly, I say to you, today you will be with me in paradise." Luke 23:43 (ESV)

He is said to have told John to take care of his mother. Talking to the two of them,

"'Woman, behold, your son!' Then he said to the disciple, 'Behold, your mother!' And from that hour the disciple took her to his own home." John 19:26-27 (ESV).

Just before Jesus' death as his final words, Matthew and Mark both say Jesus says,

"My God, my God, why have you forsaken me?" Matt 27:46 and Mark 15:34 (ESV)

He is said to say,

"I thirst." John 19:28 (ESV)

Then John says that Jesus final words are,

"It is finished." John 19:30 (ESV)

Luke says that Jesus' final words are,

"Father, into your hands I commit my spirit!" Luke 23:46 (ESV)

After this, Jesus died. John's account mentions that a soldier thrust a lance into Jesus' side to be sure he was dead, and blood and water flowed out, John 19:34. Much is written about these various accounts of what happened and what Jesus said at the end, especially the statement about God forsaking him. There are two main theories about that; some say at that moment, he is cut off from God as part of his punishment for our sins (proponents of Penal Substitution theory use this as support for the idea). Others point out that it is the beginning of Psalm 22. Reading that psalm, you will notice many parallels to what is happening to Jesus at the crucifixion. The psalm ends with,

"The generation to come will be told of the Lord, that they may proclaim to a people yet unborn the deliverance you have brought." Psalm 22:32

Maybe Jesus could not say more than that of the Psalm, but in the end, he was still teaching, and people would realize he was referring to that Psalm.

Some churches gather all these things together and think Jesus said them all. The way the accounts are written, three of the quotes above appear to be listed as his final words.

Taken together, these seven statements have been equated to the seven words: Forgiveness, Salvation, Relationship, Abandonment, Distress, Triumph, and Reunion.

Only one of the twelve disciples, John, is mentioned as being at the crucifixion. The others are said to have fled when Jesus was arrested. However, Peter and another disciple are mentioned as following to hear the trial, and Judas is mentioned as hanging himself in shame. The accounts vary, but the other followers of Jesus mentioned as present at the crucifixion are Mary, Jesus' mother, her sister, who is not named, Mary Magdalene, Mary of Clopas the mother of James the lesser and Joseph, and Salome the mother of the disciples James and John. There is much argument about the three Marys and who they all are.

In the evening, a rich man named Joseph from Arimathea, who is a follower of Jesus, asks Pilate for Jesus' body, and Pilate allows it. He wraps Jesus' body in clean linen, puts Jesus in a tomb, and rolls a huge stone across the entrance. John's account says that Nicodemus came along and helped him prepare Jesus' body according to Jewish tradition. Mary Magdalene and one of the other Marys stay there facing the tomb. The Pharisees remember that Jesus said that he would be raised from the dead on the third day, so they asked Pilate to post a guard, saying they were worried that people would steal the body and claim he was resurrected. They fix a seal on the tomb and set a guard.

The Resurrection of Jesus

The gospels vary about the story of what happened next. One says that Mary Magdalene came to the tomb on the third day, found it open, and Jesus was gone. One said that when Mary Magdalene and another Mary came, an angel appeared, rolled back the stone, and invited them to see that Jesus was gone. Another says the two Marys and Salome found the tomb open and found a man clothed in white who told them Jesus was resurrected. The other says the Marys and Joanna found the tomb open, and two men appeared and told them that Jesus was resurrected. In all accounts, they then go tell some or all the disciples. Some of the disciples go and verify this for themselves.

The accounts vary about who Jesus appeared to first. In Matthew, the eleven remaining disciples (Judas had hanged himself) went to Galilee, and they met Jesus there, and he then instructed them,

"All authority in heaven and on earth has been given to me. Go therefore and make disciples of all nations, baptizing them in the name of the Father and of the Son and of the Holy Spirit, teaching them to observe all that I have commanded you. And behold, I am with you always, to the end of the age." Matt 28:18-20 (ESV)

Mark says that Jesus first appeared to Mary Magdalene, and she went and told some of the disciples, and they did not believe her. Then he appeared in another form to two others, but the others did not believe them either. But later, he appears to the eleven disciples, saying peace be with you. He admonished them for not believing and told them,

"Go into all the world and proclaim the gospel to the whole creation. Whoever believes and is baptized will be saved, but whoever does not believe will be condemned. And these signs will accompany those who believe: in my name they will cast out demons; they will speak in new tongues; they will pick up serpents with their hands; and if they drink any deadly poison, it will not hurt them; they will lay their hands on the sick, and they will recover." Mark 16:15-18 (ESV).

Luke mentions the appearance to two of the disciples, but they do not recognize him at first because he is in a different form. Then he appeared to all the disciples, talked to them, and ate with them. He assures them that the prophecies have been fulfilled. He blesses them and then ascends to heaven.

John says that Jesus appeared first to Mary Magdalene and then later appeared to all the disciples, except Thomas, saying,

"Peace be with you. As the Father has sent me, even so I am sending you." And when he had said this, he breathed on them and said to them, 'Receive the Holy Spirit. If you forgive the sins of any, they are forgiven them; if you withhold forgiveness from any, it is withheld.'" John 20:21-23 (ESV)

Doubting Thomas does not believe them, but Jesus appears again and convinces Thomas. John mentions another time when Jesus appeared to seven of the disciples and helped them catch fish and then eats bread and fish with them. Then John says that Jesus instructed Peter to watch over his disciples and followers.

These accounts leave us to understand that Jesus instructed the disciples to go and spread his teachings and he gave them the powers to heal, cast out demons, and do other miracles.

Non-Christians do not believe the Resurrection part of the story. Still, almost all scholars admit the basic story of Jesus angering the Pharisees and them having him arrested, tried, and executed is historically true. The resurrection is a matter of faith, but belief in that is central to being a Christian.

Chapter 4: Sources

While I did not want to make this book into a dry academic paper filled with references and footnotes, I think it is important for the reader to understand the sources I used to create the book. In case you prefer not to read the details, here is a summary:

Summary

- The primary sources for the teachings of Jesus are the gospels of Matthew, Mark, Luke, and John and The Acts of the Apostles, in the New Testament. However, other New Testament books and some Old Testament books are referenced when appropriate.
- There is a dispute about when the books of the New Testament were written, with estimates ranging from 48 AD – 110 AD for various books.
- The selection of the books for inclusion in the Bible required a process over a couple of centuries and was finalized in 382 in the Council of Rome held by Pope Damasus I.
- The selected books were thought to have been written in the first century by the disciples, the apostles, or people collaborating closely with them.

- There are hundreds of articles, papers, and books discussing every aspect of the gospels and what they say. I endeavored to read many of those to help me understand and synthesize what I learned and summarize it for the reader.

Discussion

The primary sources for the teachings of Jesus are the gospels of Matthew, Mark, Luke, and John, contained in the New Testament. I do, at times, refer to other New Testament books like the Acts of the Apostles and the Letters of Paul. I also refer to some Old Testament books, mainly where Jesus referred to them. The Catholic Church and most Protestant denominations accept the teachings in these four Gospels as representative of the teachings of Jesus. However, they vary in their beliefs as to the origin and infallibility of the text in those Gospels. There are some other gospels attributed to Jesus' disciples and apostles, which were not included in the New Testament, that were also reviewed in the formulation of this book.

Unfortunately, as far as we know, Jesus did not write down his teachings, and no one that we know of followed him around and wrote them down at the time. However, multiple people wrote down his teachings later in the first century in the decades after his death, which was in about 30-33 AD. If you search the internet for "when were the gospels written," you will find many articles, papers, and books discussing this topic, and they disagree. In reading many of these sources, I found theories ranging from the first being written as early as

40 AD and other theories asserting that they were written generations later in the second century. I spent a lot of time reading various sources to determine what to summarize here. I will discuss each of the gospels below.

The Gospel of Matthew is the first book in the New Testament. It is first because when the Bible was created, it was thought to be the first one written and it was held in high esteem in the early church. Matthew was one of the original twelve disciples of Jesus. We understand that he was raised as a Jew, was well-educated, and accepted a position as a tax collector for the Roman Empire before Jesus asked Matthew to follow him. As a tax collector, he would have had to be able to read, write, and do math. It is thought that he probably could read, write, and speak Hebrew (the language used for Jewish teachings), Aramaic (the local dialect spoken in Capernaum, where he lived), Greek (the language used by the ruling Romans), and possibly some Latin (the language used by the Roman military) to be able to hold that position. The Gospel of Matthew is supposed to have been written by Matthew himself some decades after Jesus died. However, some historians think that it was written in a later generation, possibly using source material written by Matthew and based on Mark's gospel. One prominent theory is that Matthew wrote a precursor to the current gospel in 50-60 AD but in Hebrew or Aramaic, intended for use by the Jews in the region before he left to teach in other lands.

There are first and second-century historians who discuss when Matthew wrote this Gospel. For example,

Papias, the Bishop of Hierapolis (c. 60-130AD), wrote that Matthew collected the teachings of Jesus and wrote them down in Hebrew or Aramaic (there is some disagreement as to which language Papias was referring) and that *"each translated as he was able."* Papias seems to be a credible source as he sought out information from people who knew the original twelve disciples. Ireneus, a Greek Bishop (c.130-202 AD), wrote that Matthew issued a written gospel among the Hebrews in their dialect while Peter and Paul were preaching in Rome. Origen of Alexandria (c. 185-254 AD) wrote that the Gospel of Matthew was written first by Matthew. Eusebius, a Greek Historian (c. 260-339AD), wrote that Matthew wrote his gospel before he left Israel to preach in other lands, which Eusebius says happened about twelve years after the death of Jesus. This would place the writing in 42-45 AD. Jerome of Stridon (c. 342-420AD) claimed to have seen the Aramaic version. However, no known copy exists today. These historians or early church fathers wrote well after the fact, so we cannot consider these statements proof. Still, it is interesting evidence that all the early historians, even those opposed to Christianity, attribute the gospel of Matthew to Matthew himself and thought that he wrote something in the 40s AD.

Other scholars look for internal evidence in the gospel as to who wrote it and when. Every copy found contains a title or subscript attributing the gospel to Matthew, but the text itself does not describe the author. Historians point out that in 70 AD, the temple of

Jerusalem was destroyed by the Romans, yet the gospel refers to the temple in the present tense; they think this implies that it was written before 70 AD. They also point out multiple passages where the descriptions refer to monetary issues that a tax collector might find interesting. For example, when Matthew describes the Lord's Prayer that Jesus told them to pray, he says, *"and forgive us our debts,"* whereas, in the Gospel of Luke, it is recorded as *"and forgive us our sins [trespasses]."* Another example is the discussion in Matthew 17:24 between Jesus and Peter about paying taxes. They see these things as evidence that a former tax collector could have written it before 70 AD.

There are two camps in this debate. Those who say that Matthew was written in the 60s AD by Matthew and his direct followers and those who say it was written in 80-90 AD by unknown people. Given the evidence, why is there doubt today that Matthew himself wrote the Gospel of Matthew? First, no copy of the Hebrew or Aramaic version is known to exist at this point. The oldest versions or fragments of versions that we know of are from the early to mid-second century (100-200 AD) and are written in Greek. At a minimum, somebody translated Matthew's work into Greek, or alternately, somebody reworked, rewrote, or wrote the Gospel in Greek, and that is what we have today. Since Matthew likely knew Greek, he could have been the person who created the Greek version, but we have no evidence one way or the other about Matthew's direct involvement.

So, the Gospel of Matthew could be an eyewitness

account of Jesus' teaching written by Matthew himself. It could also be a secondhand account written by followers of Matthew, based on Matthew's eyewitness account and his teachings. Or it could have been written later based on oral tradition, Mark's Gospel, and unknown sources, finally written down and attributed to Matthew. We simply do not know for sure.

I do not want to bore the reader, so I will not go into as much detail with the other three Gospels as I did with the Gospel of Matthew, but hopefully, that discussion gives the reader the flavor for the types of discussions that swirl around this topic. Instead, I will summarize what I found about the rest of them.

The Gospel of Mark is supposed to have been written by a person named John Mark. John Mark was not one of the original twelve disciples but may have been one of the seventy-two [or seventy] apostles sent out by Jesus to spread his teachings (Luke 10:1). Mark is said to have been an interpreter, companion, and follower of one of the original twelve disciples, Peter, and a companion of Paul an apostle of Jesus who authored many books in the New Testament. Many historians think that the Gospel of Mark was the first one written. There are two communities of scholars, those who date it to 40-60 AD and others 60-70 AD. Some of the same scholars who doubt Matthew's involvement in that gospel assert that the Gospel of Mark was written later by anonymous people. There is unanimous agreement in the writings of early historians and church fathers that John Mark, a companion of Peter, wrote this Gospel. It is unclear if

John Mark was an eyewitness to any of Jesus' teachings, but he certainly had access to people who were. So, this gospel is, at best, a secondhand account using firsthand witnesses as sources.

The Gospel of Luke (also Acts) is believed to have been written by a physician and companion of the apostle Paul. Paul was not one of the original twelve disciples; he converted after Jesus died. But is said to have spent some time with Peter, the disciple, and James, Jesus' brother. So, it is possible that Luke met some of the disciples. Scholars' opinions differ as to when it was written. Reviewing the literature, they range from as early as 58 AD and as late as 110 AD, but most place it between 80-90 AD. Luke is supposed to have lived to eighty-four and died late in the first century, so these dates are possible. The text asserts that the author investigated the events accurately and mentions eyewitness accounts handed down to him (Luke 1:2-3). Hence, this Gospel represents a second or thirdhand account of the life and teachings of Jesus using eyewitness accounts.

The Gospel of John is thought to have been written by one of the original twelve disciples of Jesus. John was a fisherman called by Jesus to follow him. Many scholars believe that John did not write it himself but that his followers wrote it based on John's teachings. They support this view by pointing out that it was written in well-written Greek, and they doubt that a simple fisherman in that area could speak or write Greek. So, the Gospel of John could be an eyewitness account of

Jesus' teachings or a secondhand account based on eyewitness accounts from John himself. Scholars date its current form to 90-110 AD but admit that some may have been written as early as 70 AD, possibly dictated by John to a follower who could read and write Greek. John is believed to have lived to 100 AD and also wrote some of the Catholic Epistles and the book of Revelation.

Paul is thought to have written or dictated to scribes thirteen books of the New Testament, all in the form of letters to various groups of Christians. The books are Romans, 1 and 2 Corinthians, Galatians, Ephesians, Philippians, Colossians, 1 and 2 Thessalonians, 1 and 2 Timothy, Titus, and Philemon. They were all supposed to have been written by Paul with the help of scribes as necessary throughout his ministry between 50 and 67 AD. Paul wrote other letters that are not included in the Bible as well. The authorship of Romans, 1 and 2 Corinthians, Galatians, Philippians, 1 Thessalonians, and Philemon are generally undisputed as written by Paul in that time period. The letters to the Ephesians, Colossians, and 2 Thessalonians are sometimes referred to as Deutero-Pauline and are disputed by some scholars who think Paul's followers wrote them in 70-80 AD. Some scholars assert that Paul or his direct followers did not write the letters 1 and 2 Timothy and Titus, which were written to individuals and deviated from Paul's style and teachings in the other letters. They propose dates for these from 80-100 AD. Hebrews is sometimes associated with Paul, but it is more like a sermon, and its authorship is unknown; it is dated from 80-90 AD.

After spending many hours reading about the origins of the Gospels and the other books, it is impossible not to notice that secular sources assert that the Gospels were written generations after Jesus died by anonymous people who they say made up much of it to elevate the religion. They say these anonymous writings circulated around the Roman Empire for a century or more before they were attributed to the current authors.

They assert that Jesus could not foresee future events, so if he predicted an event that later happened, like the temple's destruction in 70 AD, they use that as evidence that the text was written after the event. This is a particularly flimsy argument. Predicting that the Romans would eventually destroy the temple would not require divine powers. Anyone noticing how the Jews chafed under Roman rule could have predicted the Jews would rebel, and the Romans would respond in force.

The Gospels of Matthew, Mark, and Luke contain many similarities and are referred to as the synoptic Gospels. This means that taken together they present a summary of Jesus life and teachings. There are many theories about how that happened. Most scholars think that Matthew and Luke both used Mark as a source and also added unique material. In fact, over 90% of the content of Luke is also in Matthew and over 50% of the content in Mark is found in Luke. All but about three percent of the content of Mark appears in either Matthew or Luke. There is also content in common between Matthew and Luke that is not in Mark and unique material in Matthew and Luke.

There is a popular theory known as the *Two-source Theory* (Christian Hermann Weisse, 1838) that there was another early source that was a collection of Jesus' sayings, now lost, named "Q." Some scholars theorize that Matthew and Luke used "Q" in addition to Mark as sources, but that Luke and Matthew were written independently. Some scholars suggest that "Q" could be the earlier writings of Matthew in Hebrew or Aramaic and that Matthew, Mark, and Luke, all used it as a source.

A popular competing view is the *Farrer Hypothesis* (Austin Farrer, 1955) that proposes that Mark was written first, then Matthew was written using most of Mark plus original material. Then Luke was written pulling from both Mark and Matthew and adding original material. This hypothesis eliminates the need for the Q source.

There is another hypotheses called the *Augustinian hypothesis* (St. Augustine bishop of Hippo, c. 400 AD) that Matthew was written first, and Mark pulled from Matthew, not the other way around. Then Luke was written pulling from Matthew and Mark. Other hypotheses exist as well.

These views are all speculative. All we can say for sure is that there is a lot of similarity between these three Gospels. It is not hard to believe that these authors would have shared information or borrowed from each other or other sources and after all, they were writing about the same events.

Some believers go to great lengths to show that the Gospels could have been written in the mid-first century by the original disciples or their followers and that they attempted to document the true story. One author, Dr. Brant Pitre, *"The Case for Jesus,"* 2016, that I found particularly convincing, pointed out that every early copy we have of these gospels (there are hundreds of them) attributes them to the four authors mentioned above. No anonymous copies have ever been found. Dr. Pitre says, suppose they were anonymous and circulating for a century before being attributed to these authors. Wouldn't there be copies of these anonymous writings or copies attributed to other people? There are none. Also, wouldn't there be second or third-century scholars expressing their doubts about the origins of the Gospels? I looked for them, and I could find none.

Like Dr. Pitre, before doing this research, I had pretty much accepted the assertion that the gospels were anonymous in origin, written generations after Jesus died. I did believe that the people who wrote them were attempting to record the events of Jesus' life and his teachings accurately, but I had concerns about how accurate they could be generations later. After doing this research, I am beginning to believe it is possible that the Gospels were written by Matthew, Mark, Luke, and John or by their immediate followers using Matthew, Mark, Luke, and John themselves as sources, not generations later. As to the accuracy and truthfulness of what they wrote, that is impossible to verify and is a matter of faith.

I encourage the readers to go on their own voyage of discovery and decide for themselves what they think about the origins of the Gospels.

As for the other Gospels and books not included in the Bible, like the Gospels of Thomas, Philip, and Mary and as many as 49 other books that were considered, the first question that occurred was, "Why were they not included versus the 27 books that were included in the New Testament." I had been previously led to believe that it was all political or that they contained secrets that the church did not want to reveal. However, I learned that most of the books that were not chosen were thought to be written in the second or third century or were of unknown origin, ruling them out as being written by the apostles or their direct followers. Simply put, those books did not appear to go back to the earliest generation and thus were less trusted or accepted. The accepted books were thought to come from the first century and to be written by the disciples, the apostles, or people collaborating closely with them. Also, widespread use and acceptance was a factor in their selection.

There were some books that almost made it, like the *Didache,* which is anonymous in origin and claims to be "The teaching of the Lord to the Gentiles (or Nations) by the twelve apostles." It reads like an instruction manual for people to live by and has much in common with Matthew and Luke. Many theorize that it was a derivative work of Matthew and Luke. Those reasons may be why it was not selected. Another example is *1 Clement,* a letter written by Pope St. Clement I to the church of Corinth in the first century. It is more about the early church than the life and teaching of Jesus. There are quite a few others that are thought to be writings of the Apostolic Fathers and are considered to be valuable early Christian works but were not chosen to be included in the Bible as scripture. There are numerous books available that include and discuss these writings. Religious scholars study the writings of the Apostolic Fathers and the Bible to gain valuable insights. I read *"The Apostolic Fathers in English"* by Michael W. Holmes 2006 to learn about these works.

In the early 300s, according to Bishop Eusebius of Caesarea's *"Church History,"* the possible books were divided into categories of accepted, disputed, or rejected by orthodox Christians. The classifications of various books were much debated at the time. The Council of Nicaea in 325 AD was the first ecumenical council or meeting of the bishops and other authorities of the church. It defined Christian doctrine and created the Nicene Creed, but it did not finalize the selection of books for the Bible. The matter was decided in 382 AD at the Council of Rome held by Pope Damasus I, and the list of accepted Old Testament and New Testament books was finalized. The Catholic Church still accepts that list today. Protestants have removed seven books from the accepted list of Old Testament books, which explains some of the differences between Catholics and Protestants. For example, the existence of Purgatory is supported by the mention of praying for the dead, which is in the Book of Maccabees in the Catholic Old

Testament and not the Protestant version. The New Testaments contain the same books in the Catholic and Protestant Bible versions.

As far as the Gospel of Mary goes, the first issue is that much of it has not survived. A copy was first discovered in 1896, written in Coptic and bound with other early Christian Gnostic texts. The copy found is thought to have been created in the late fourth or early fifth century. Two other fragments have been found written in Greek and are from the third century. Pages 1-6 and 11-14 are missing; perhaps someday, a full version will be found. Second, it is thought to have been initially written in the second or third century. I did not find any scholars suggesting an earlier date for that text. Given that, it was not written by any Mary from Jesus' time. Third, there is disagreement as to which Mary it refers. There are six women named Mary mentioned in the Bible related to Jesus. Many say it is Mary Magdalene, but the text does not say that. Some suggest it is Jesus' mother Mary, and others suggest Mary of Bethany or Mary a sister of Jesus. The surviving text starts after the crucifixion and resurrection of Jesus. It asserts that Jesus loved Mary the most and gave her unique teaching that he did not mention to the other disciples. The surviving part talks about what happens when the soul ascends to heaven and how it is challenged by various mystic powers on the way. The text says that two of the disciples, Andrew and Peter, told her they did not believe that Jesus told her these things, and if the conversation ever took place, they did not pass these teachings on.

This gospel is viewed by the early church as Gnostic and of questionable origin. The earliest references to it by the church fathers are in the third century. I could not find evidence that the Gospel of Mary was rejected or even known in 382 AD at the Council of Rome held by Pope Damasus I. I also could not find evidence that the Gospel of Mary was rejected for patriarchal reasons either; that is just conjecture.

There are many other second or third-century writings that are not part of the Bible. They were not selected for inclusion in the Bible because they were not from the first century, and some were of questionable origins. At this point, the New Testament and the writings of the Apostolic Fathers are the primary accepted sources of our understanding of Jesus and his Teachings. Those who are especially curious might go and read the writings of the Apostolic Fathers, the books excluded from the Protestant Old Testament, and other excluded books to add to their understanding. Hopefully, this section gives the reader an idea of how we arrived at the current bible. Could politics have played a role? Certainly, it could have, but it seems to me that there was an honest attempt by faithful people to choose the most authoritative and accepted books from the first century to be included in the Bible. Some people believe that divine inspiration guided the choices, but that again, is a matter of faith.

Chapter 5: Versions of the Bible

There are over one hundred complete English translations of the Bible and thousands of versions in various languages. This section discusses the difficulties related to the existence of all those versions and which versions I used.

Summary

- Multiple bible versions were consulted in the creation of this book, often using online sources like Bible Gateway that make it easy to compare over sixty translations.
- The versions quoted are:
  - The *New American Bible Revised Edition NABRE* is a new translation from the oldest sources.
  - The *English Standard Version ESV* is rooted in the *King James Version KJV* with many rounds of corrections (see the discussion below.)
- In this book, I marked each quote showing which translation I quoted with NABRE or ESV. In each case, I picked a translation that agreed with most translations and avoided minority translations.

- When substantive differences exist between these two, I quote one and show the difference in braces [like this].

Discussion

What version/translation of the Bible should we read? There are hundreds of versions, and they have small to significant differences. This topic could fill a book on its own, and it is a highly politically charged topic. One problem is that the Bible was written 1900 years ago or more. The Old Testament was written in ancient Hebrew and Aramaic, and the New Testament was written in ancient Greek. Most people do not read those languages, nor do we know how the words were used at the time. We must rely on language scholars to do the best job possible to translate to our language without changing the meaning.

If you have studied other languages, you have encountered situations where there is no direct translation for a word or phrase. For example, in English, when somebody says *thank you*, we say *you're welcome*. In Spanish, when somebody says *gracias*, which means *thank you*, they say *de nada*. However, *de nada* translates literally to *it's nothing*. The meanings are similar, but *you're welcome*, and *it's nothing* have slightly different meanings. You could also use *mucho gusto*, which means *with pleasure*, or *esta bien*, which means *it's all good*, or *con gusto*, which means *happy to help*, all of which are different from *you're welcome*. So different translators might choose differently when translating *you're welcome* to Spanish. Many such choices had to be made when translating ancient Hebrew, Aramaic, and Greek into English. The article "*A Closer Look at 'Word for Word' Bible Translation*" by Lora Gilb posted on the web site *Patterns of Evidence* discusses several such translation issues in translating Greek words in the Bible into English.

There are no known original versions of any of the books of the Bible. All translations published today are based on versions that were copies of copies handed down through the ages. The more times the text is copied, the more opportunities there are for changes to creep in. The oldest copies that we can unearth have the highest likelihood of being close to the original since they would have been copied fewer times. Recent archaeo-logical finds have uncovered ancient copies and fragments of copies from the second and third centuries. The fragments are important as they can be translated and used to reconstruct earlier text and correct portions of later versions. Papyrus, made from the spongy material in the stems of the papyrus plants, was used like paper in the first century. It is durable if kept very dry but can deteriorate rapidly in moist climates. It can also become fragile if it is used frequently. So, many ancient papyrus manuscripts are damaged or have deteriorated completely.

The list of books chosen for the New Testament was not finalized until 382 AD, so complete copies of the New Testament in its current form were not produced until after that. The Codex Sinaiticus, written in Greek from 325-350 AD, contains all the books in the current New

Testament, plus other books. It was written on vellum, which is based on animal skins, and may be the earliest copy of all the books that were later chosen for the New Testament, all in one book. When I mention translations from the earliest sources, it is sources like the Codex Sinaiticus, and many of the fragments mentioned, as well as Latin versions commissioned by Pope Damasus I in 382 AD, that were used.

In my naive state, I went to Google and asked, "What is the most accurate translation of the bible"? That was quite an education! There are word-for-word, phrase-for-phrase, or formal equivalence translations, meaning-for-meaning or closest natural equivalence translations, thought-for-thought or so-called functional equivalence translations, and paraphrase or retelling translations. Translating things word-for-word can result in odd phrasing and hard-to-read text. Phrase-for-phrase seems like a better model, which better describes what many translators did. The concern with meaning-for-meaning, thought-for-thought, and paraphrase translations is that while they are easier to read, the translator determines the meaning and writes that in the new language when there may very well be different interpretations possible in the original. It seems better if the ambiguity comes through in the translation so the reader can decide.

The King James Version KJV was a very influential early translation of the Bible into English. It was created in the early 1600s and was commissioned by King James VI of England for the Church of England. The translators did not use ancient versions of the Bible as their source. They are thought to have used Greek Versions available from the 1500s, like the Textus Receptus, and then existing translations in various languages as their sources, like the Geneva Bible, the Bishop's Bible, and others. For the Old Testament they are thought to have used a Hebrew Rabbinic Bible from the 1500s and some Greek and Latin versions. The problem is that those versions had been copied and re-copied for over a thousand years, and additions, changes, and deletions had crept in. When ancient versions of the Bible were discovered and translated, hundreds of differences were found compared to the King James version.

While the King James version was a good-faith effort, it was based on sources that had drifted from the original because of accumulated errors and changes of many centuries of manuscript copying. When this was realized, multiple efforts were undertaken to correct the errors, resulting in numerous newer versions.

The version my church used when I was young was the "Revised Standard Version" RSV, which was based on the "American Standard Version" ASV from 1901, which was a revision of the King James version from 1611. Revisions occurred in 1881-1885, then again in 1901, and again in 1945-1951 based on comparisons with ancient versions. More recently, efforts have been undertaken to retranslate the Bible from the most ancient versions available to produce versions as close to the original as possible rather than trying to correct an older translation. Given its longevity, the KJV is the most widely owned and read English version in the US. However, many churches have moved away from KJV, and it is not currently the most widely sold version.

According to the Evangelical Christian Publishers Association ECPA, for over twenty-five years, the best-selling English translation of the Bible is the *New International Version NIV*, described as "a completely original translation of the Bible developed by more than one hundred scholars working from the best available Hebrew, Aramaic, and Greek texts." It is somewhere between a word-for-word or literal and thought-for-thought translation.

Others frequently mentioned in the top ten are (removing two that are not in English):

King James Version KJV, which is the original version from 1611 with changes to update spelling, grammar, and punctuation that has changed in the English language.

The *English Standard Version ESV,* a newer revision of the RSV. It is described as a word-for-word or formal equivalence translation. It has its roots in the KJV but has been updated many times, and the publishers say it was "created by a team of more than 100 leading evangelical scholars and pastors." Interestingly, on Amazon, the search term "best-selling bible" shows the ESV Study Bible first.

New Living Translation NLT dynamic equivalence or thought-for-thought translation from the best available Hebrew, Aramaic, and Greek texts.

Christian Standard Bible CSB is a thought-for-thought or optimal equivalence translation. Translated by an international team of one hundred scholars from seventeen de-nominations, from Hebrew, Aramaic, and Greek texts.

New King James Version NKJV, an updated version of KJV to modern English. *New Living Translation NLT* dynamic equivalence or thought-for-thought translation.

New American Standard Bible NASB is touted as the most literally translated.

New Revised Standard Version NRSV is another more recent revision of the RSV and has both Protestant and Catholic versions.

Most Protestant denominations do not pick a standard version; they allow each church to choose. Most of the versions listed above are widely used.

For Catholics in the United States, the Catholic Bible Press lists these two bible versions:

The *New American Bible* revised edition from 2011, *NABRE,* is the official Catholic version in the United States. It is authorized by the US Conference of Catholic Bishops and is "Translated from the Original Languages with Critical Use of All the Ancient Sources." It is described as a formal equivalence translation. The readings at mass, the Lectionary, are currently based on the previous edition of the *New American Bible,* NAB, not the NABRE, but an update of the Lectionary is in progress.

The *New Revised Standard Version, Catholic Edition NRSV-CE*, is also an official bible of the Catholic Church and is approved by the United States Conference of Catholic Bishops and the Canadian Conference of Catholic Bishops. It has its roots in the KJV but was updated based on *"the latest archaeological discoveries, including the Dead Sea Scrolls, early Greek manuscripts, and recent updates in Semitic language studies. The old English pronouns and verbs were updated to current English."*

There are many other popular bible versions not mentioned. Such a dizzying array of versions makes it challenging to decide which to read. For this book, I preferred to use a recent translation from the earliest sources and one rooted in the KJV with corrections. I also lean towards the more literal translations. Multiple versions were consulted to understand Jesus' teachings. However, the *NABRE,* a new translation from the oldest sources, and the *ESV*, a much-updated version of the *KJV,* were used for all citations. However, I found www.biblegateway.com to be a terrific way to compare any given passage across many different translations.

One key point to make here is that it seems extremely unlikely that any existing version of the Bible in any language is 100% accurate in rendering the original writings or the exact teachings of Jesus. First, Jesus likely spoke in Aramaic and possibly Greek, and nobody wrote down what he said word for word. At best, his disciples or their followers wrote the gospels ten to fifty years after Jesus died from their memory of what he said.

It would have helped their memories that they repeated his teachings over and over when they taught, but it is unlikely they could remember exactly, word for word, what he said. This is reflected in differences in descriptions of the same events in different gospels (compare the Lord's Prayer in Matthew 6.9–13 and Luke 11.1–4, for example.) They also translated Jesus' Aramaic teachings into Greek. Right from the beginning, there are two possible sources of error: human memory and translation difficulties. Then, add possible errors in the process of making copies by hand and later errors in translation to English, unintended or intended. So, what are we to do? I think that we should read Jesus' teachings across multiple translations of the Gospels, read learned analyses of those teachings, figure out the big picture, and accept that the small details are debatable. That is what I did in this book.

Epilogue

I have endeavored to faithfully summarize the life, death, and teachings of Jesus. For those who read this hoping to learn more about Jesus and his teachings, I hope I have accomplished that. A summary leaves out many details; for those who now thirst for more detail, that is good; then seek, and you shall find. There are many other books, and of course, there is the Bible itself. If I have inspired you to learn more, that makes me happy. If you are upset that I have omitted some favorite detail or something you think is a key point, I am sorry. I cannot include everything without just duplicating the whole Bible. However, I am open to amending the book in the future if you convince me it is necessary.

If one church or another is upset that I have not upheld their version of beliefs, know that doing so was not my purpose. I was trying to represent Jesus' teachings correctly as I understood them after reading the Bible and many other sources. I believe that it would be immoral of me to misrepresent Jesus' teaching to support the views of one church or another. Please do not label me a heretic and seek to punish me.

This has been an interesting journey for me. My understanding of Jesus and his teachings has changed significantly from what it was before authoring this book. I now have a deeper and more positive understanding, but I realize it could take a lifetime of study and contemplation to claim complete understanding.

Fortunately, Jesus did not say that complete understanding is required for salvation. If you are still unclear on what is required, please reread the section on salvation. While some people might say not all that is mentioned in that section is required, if you do those things, according to my understanding of Jesus' teachings, he said that you will surely be saved.

The Disciples

Throughout the New Testament, the twelve disciples are integral to the teachings of Jesus. Many of Jesus' teachings come from discussions with the disciples or are in response to questions from the disciples. Also, the disciples are witnesses to his teachings, and they are the source of our knowledge about them.

The disciples led the efforts to spread what Jesus taught after his death. According to tradition, the disciples mostly stayed in Judea for ten to twelve years. The Bible mentions seventy-two disciples (Luke 10) and later one hundred and twenty disciples (Acts 1:15), so there were many other followers of Jesus who were sent out to spread his teachings. Peter presided over the Council of Jerusalem in the early days of the church, as mentioned in Acts 15. Around 41-44 AD, Herod Agrippa, the grandson of Herod the Great, started to persecute Christians to curry favor with the Jews. Some of the original twelve were killed early. Many of the others eventually left and traveled to various places, teaching and establishing churches, and most were eventually martyred for their faith.

The disciples are listed in Matt 10:2-4, Mark 3:16-18, Luke 6:14-15 and Acts 1:13. Many of these details are Church tradition, not documented history. I found some of the church lore on the Catholic Answers web site and in the Catholic Encyclopedia. Their names are:

- **Simon**, who is called **Simon Peter** or just **Peter** since there is another Simon. He was a fisherman, born in Bethsaida, and settled in a home with his brother in Capernaum. He is Andrew's older brother, and they worked with James and John. He was a natural leader and was the one Jesus called the rock upon which he would build his church. He denies knowing Jesus three times when he is caught trying to hear Jesus's trial, as Jesus predicted. He was married. He led the early church for about 15 years after Jesus' death. John was imprisoned by Herod when Herod killed James, but an Angel rescued John. After that, he is thought to have taught in various places. According to church lore, he is believed to have been captured and killed in Rome during the reign of Nero around 67 AD.

- **Andrew** was the brother of Simon Peter and had the same background. He was a follower of John the Baptist. He was the first to follow Jesus and was there when John baptized Jesus. He introduced Peter to Jesus. According to church lore, he was sent to teach along the shores of the Black Sea in current-day Greece and Turkey and was killed in Patras, Greece, around 61 AD.

- **James**, a fisherman and son of Zebedee. John is his younger brother. James and his brother often argued, and Jesus nicknamed them the Sons of Thunder. James is thought to have taught in Spain. Herod Agrippa killed him with a sword, about 42-44 AD (Acts 12:1-3)

- **John**, a fisherman and son of Zebedee. James is his older brother. Called the "disciple Jesus loved" in the Gospel of John. Thought to have been a follower of John the Baptist. Credited with writing the Gospel, 1, 2, and 3 John letters, and the book of Revelations. He was exiled to the island of Patmos by the Romans but later went to Ephesus and governed churches. He is thought to have lived to around 98-100 AD and died of natural causes in Ephesus.

- **Philip**, we do not know much about him before being called. Some scholars think he was a follower of John the Baptist. According to church lore, he taught in Greece, Syria, and Asia Minor and died in Hierapolis in Persia around 62 AD.

- **Bartholomew**, also known as **Nathanael**, came from Cana in Galilee (John 21:2) and may have preached in India. One story says he was killed while serving the people of Albinopolis, Armenia, around 72 AD, but that is not widely accepted.

- **Thomas** was nicknamed "Doubting Thomas," also called "the Twin" of whom we do not know. Thought to have taught in several places, started the Christian church in India, and was killed by a form of crucifixion around 60 AD in India.

- **Matthew** was also referred to as Levi because he was a Levite. He was a tax collector for the Romans and was well off financially. Credited with writing the Gospel of Matthew. One story says he taught in Ethiopia and Egypt. Hircanus, the King of some part of Ethiopia, had him killed with a spear about 65 AD.

- **James**, the son of Alphaeus, his mother is named Mary, and he has a brother named Joseph, but we do not know much else. He was referred to as James the younger or less in Mark 15:40. Tradition says he was the Bishop of Jerusalem and was killed in Jerusalem in 62 AD.

- **Thaddaus**, also known as Judas son of James, Jude, and Lebbaeus. Early tradition says that he visited Edessa. There, he healed the King of Edessa, Abgar. The traditional symbol of Thaddaus is a club, and tradition says he was clubbed to death for his faith around 67 AD in Persia.

- **Simon** the Zealot was a political activist. Not much is known, and he is placed in various legends in the Middle East, Africa, and as far away as England. Thought to have been killed in Edessa, Greece, around the year 67 AD.

- **Judas** Iscariot, not much is known. He betrayed Jesus for thirty pieces of silver. According to Matthew, he hanged himself in shame. Acts says he fell from a height and died.

- **Matthias**, according to Acts, was a follower of Jesus from the beginning and was chosen by the then one hundred and twenty disciples to replace Judas

Iscariot in the twelve. Tradition says he went to teach in what is now the country of Georgia and was killed in about 65 AD.

Peter, John, and James the son of Zebedee, are thought to be the inner circle. They were the only ones with Jesus when he raised a girl from the dead (Mark 5:37) and were with Jesus at the transfiguration on a high mountain (Matt 17:1)

Definitions

These definitions relate to the meanings of the words in Jesus' time and as used in the scriptures.

Apocryphal – Something of doubtful authenticity, but that may be widely circulated as being true.

Apostle – An apostle is one who is sent out to spread the teachings of Jesus. The twelve disciples became apostles when Jesus sent them out to spread his teachings.

Catholic - derived from the Greek word katholikos, meaning "universal." First used in relation to the church in *"The Epistle of Ignatius to the Smyrnaeans"* Ch. 8 c. 110 AD.

Decapolis – An area north of Perea, east of Samaria, and the Jordan River. Jesus visited some places in Decapolis in his ministry.

Disciple – A disciple of Jesus is someone who followed Jesus and learned from him. Jesus had many disciples; some were sent out to spread his teachings and could then be described as apostles.

Exegetical - a critical interpretation or explanation of text, especially scriptures, to determine their meaning.

High Priests – Priests who ran the temple and were selected from the priests annually. They could be members of the Sadducees but less likely Pharisees.

Galilee – At the time of Jesus, an area north of Samaria and west of the Sea of Galilee. Jesus grew up in Nazareth in Galilee. Much of Jesus' early ministry takes place in Galilee.

Gaulanitis – an area east of Galilee, north of Decapolis. Jesus visited some places in Gaulanitis in his ministry.

Gnostic – In the first and second centuries after the life of Jesus, Gnostics believed in personal spiritual knowledge and mystical practices instead of the church's emerging orthodox beliefs and practices.

Judea – at the time of Jesus, it was a Roman Province, the area between the Mediterranean Sea and the Dead Sea up to Bethel in the north and the Negeb Desert in the south. Jerusalem and Bethlehem are in Judea.

Nomina Sacra – Abbreviations of "sacred names" and titles used by ancient scribes in ancient Christian manuscripts.

Palestine – At the time of Jesus, it was an area controlled by the Roman Empire between Syria to the North and Egypt to the South, including the areas named Judea, Idumea, Samaria, Galilee, Perea, Decapolis, Batanea, and others. Judea, Galilee, and Perea were the main Jewish areas.

Peraea – An area east of the Dead Sea and the Jordan River east of northern Judea and Samaria. Jesus is described in the Gospels as traveling through Perea to go to Jerusalem.

Pharisees - Members of a Jewish sect or political party interested in strict observance of rites, traditions, and ceremonies based on the oral traditions of the fathers, not just the Torah. They were frequently in conflict with the Sadducees. They were not generally nobility but were often influential people. The Pharisees continued to exist after the Romans destroyed the temple in Jerusalem, but that term faded away, and they are said to have evolved into the rabbinic movement.

Phoenicia – An area north of Galilee, Jesus visited some places in Phoenicia in his ministry.

Porneia (πορνεία) - at the time of Jesus, meant any sexual relations outside of marriage or any form of illicit sexual intercourse, including prostitution, adultery, pedophilia, homosexuality, lesbianism, incest, fornication (sex between unmarried people), and bestiality. (Greek Lexicon :: Strong's G4202)

Priests – trained religious leaders required to officiate at various rituals, offerings, and blessings. They all had to be from the tribe of Levites descended from Aaron.

Prodigal – wasteful, extravagant, spending money recklessly.

Rabbi – A respectful term for a teacher. At the time, it was not formalized or reserved for officially ordained people as it is today. Jesus was called rabbi multiple times by various people in the Bible; he was called a teacher often as well.

Sadducees - Members of a Jewish sect who emphasized strict observance of the Torah over oral tradition. They were often priests or members of the nobility or wealthy families. They were frequently in conflict with the Pharisees. After the Romans destroyed the temple in Jerusalem in 70 AD, this sect soon ceased to exist.

Samaria – at the time of Jesus, north of Judea, between the Mediterranean Sea and the Jordan River up to just south of Nazareth. Jesus visited some places in Samaria in his ministry.

Sanhedrin – A ruling council for the Jewish people, subservient to the Roman rulers. It functioned as the courts and as an administrative body. At the local level, there were "lesser Sanhedrins" of twenty-three members in each town with at least 120 adult males and a central "great Sanhedrin" of seventy-one members. Cases could be tried in lesser Sanhedrin and appealed to the greater one. The members were nobility and could include Priests, Scribes, and lay elders.

Scribe - Men who had knowledge of the Hebrew law and could draft legal documents like contracts for marriages, loans, sales of land, etc. They studied the scriptures to understand the Jewish laws and were also teachers of the law. They could also be members of the Sadducees or Pharisees sects. Most of them were killed when the Jews rebelled against the Romans (66-70 AD)

Synagogue – a Jewish church. Any adult member of the community could deliver short sermons. Jesus is mentioned as teaching in synagogues many times in the Bible, but he also taught in other places. A person called the hazzan was responsible for the synagogue, arranging services, caring for the Torah scrolls, etc. Some rituals could only be performed if a priest was present, but priests did not run the synagogues.

Transliterate – Translate a word into another language using the letters in the destination language that are closest to the letters in the original language. Often used for names. This is different from translation, where words are translated to the word with the same meaning in the destination language.

References

Bibles Quoted

The New American Bible, Revised Edition, NABRE, Confraternity of Christian Doctrine, 2010, 1991, 1986, 1970, Washington, DC.

Holy Bible. English Standard Version, ESV, Crossway, a publishing ministry of Good News Publishers, 2001, Wheaton, Illinois.

Holy Bible, King James Version, KJV, (Originally published 1611)

Other References Mentioned

St. Augustine, *De Consensu Evangelistarum (aka The Harmony of the Gospels,) c. 400.* (origin of the Augustinian hypothesis.)

Broussard, Karlo. *Purgatory Is for Real: Good News About the Afterlife for Those Who Aren't Perfect Yet*, Catholic Answers Press, 2020, El Cajon, California.

Durant, Will. *Caesar and Christ A History of Roman Civilization and of Christianity from the beginnings to AD 325"*, Simon and Schuster, 1944, New York.

Eusebius, Bishop of Caesarea. *Church History*, c. fifth century.

Farrer, Austin M., *On Dispensing with Q*, in D. E. Nineham (ed.), *Studies in the Gospels*, Oxford: Blackwell, 1955, pp. 55-86. (Origin of the Farrer Hypothesis.)

Gertoux, Gerard. *Herod the Great and Jesus: Chronological, Historical and Archaeological Evidence*, Lulu.com, 2015, Raleigh, NC.

Holmes. Michael W. *The Apostolic Fathers in English*, Baker Academic, 2006, Grand Rapids, MI. (Contains 1 Clement and The Didache mentioned in this book)

Horsley, Richard A. *Galilee: History, Politics, People*, Trinity, 1995, Valley Forge, Penn.

Map derived from: Kent, C. F. (1906) *Palestine in the time of Jesus, 4 B.C. - 30 A.D.: including the period of Herod, 40 - 4 B.C.* [S.l.: s.n] [Map] Retrieved from the Library of Congress, https://www.loc.gov/item/2009579463/, Public Domain

Pitre, Brant. *The Case for Jesus: The Biblical and Historical Evidence for Christ*, The Crown Publishing Group, 2016, New York.

Taylor, Joan E. *What did Jesus Look Like?*, Bloomsbury T&T Clark, 2018, London.

Weisse, Christian Hermann, *Two-source hypothesis*, 1838, Possibly first published in the journal, *Zeitschrift für Philosophie und philosophische Kritik*, ed Hermann Fichte.

Unknown, *"The Gospel of Mary" Berlin Gnostic Codex (Papyrus Berolinensis 8502)*, c. third century.

Unknown, *"Infancy Gospel of Thomas" Codex Tchacos*, c. late second century.

Unknown, *"Gospel of James" Papyrus Bodmer 5*, c. 150 AD.

Scholars Specifically Referenced

Celsus was a Greek or Roman philosopher in the second century. He wrote *"The True Word"* around 170-180 AD. It is the first known significant work critical of Christianity. This work is useful in confirming what early Christians believed through the lens of a non-believer. It confirms that early Christians believed in the virgin birth of Jesus, that he said he was the son of God, that Jesus performed miracles, and that he died and was resurrected.

Clement of Alexandria (c. 150-215 AD) was a Christian theologian and philosopher. Considered to be a Church Father. Wrote *The Protrepticus* (c. 195 AD), *The Paedagogus* (c. 198 AD), and *The Stromata* (c.198-203 AD), which are all considered to be important early Christian writings. He is considered to be an early Church Father.

Cornelius Tacitus (c. 56-120 AD) was a Roman historian and politician. His work includes one of the earliest references to the crucifixion of Jesus outside the Bible.

Dionysius Exiguus was a Scythian monk who produced the BC/AD system in 525 AD.

Eusebius of Caesarea (c. 260-339AD) was a Greek or Palestinian historian and Bishop of Caesarea in Roman Syria who wrote multiple works on the gospels. Considered to be an early church father.

Flavius Josephus (37-100 AD) was a Jewish historian. He recorded details about events in the first century that confirm some of the details in the Bible about Pontius Pilate, Herod the Great, John the Baptist, James, brother of Jesus, and Jesus of Nazareth in his work *"Antiquities of the Jews"* (c. 94 AD).

Ireneus, a Greek Bishop (c. 130-202 AD), was noted for expanding Christianity in southern France and developing Christian Theology.

Jerome of Stridon (c. 342-420) was a Catholic Priest, theologian, and historian. He is known for his translation of the Bible into Latin.

John A. Cramer is a physics professor at Oglethorpe University in Atlanta, Georgia. Wrote a letter to the Biblical Archaeology Society (BAR) in 2013 in response to an article about the date of Herod's death that is used to determine when Jesus was born. He points out that other Eclipses might better fit the historical account.

Justin Martyr (100-165 AD) was a Greek philosopher and early supporter of Christianity. He is known as the first Christian apologist, which means "to defend with speech." He wrote and spoke in support of Christianity and was beheaded by the Romans for refusing to make sacrifices to the Roman gods. He is considered to be an early Church Father.

Origen of Alexandria (c. 185-254AD) was an early Christian theologian and biblical scholar. He is one of the early church fathers. He wrote hundreds of treatises and commentaries about Christianity. He extensively refutes Celsus' work, and his work provides insights into early Christianity. He is considered to be an early Church Father.

Papias, the Bishop of Hierapolis (c. 60-130AD), is considered an early church father. Often cited as a source related to early church tradition and the origin of the gospels.

St. Hippolytus of Rome (c. 170-235 AD) was an important second-third-century Christian theologian and is considered to be an early Church Father.

St. Epiphanius of Salamis (c, 310-403 AD) was the bishop of Salamis, Cyprus. He was a defender of the Christian faith and is considered to be an early Church Father.

Theophilus of Antioch (c. 169-183 AD) was a Bishop of Antioch and authored books defending Christianity.

Thomas Aquinas (1225-1274AD) was an Italian Dominican friar and priest known for his commentaries on Christian doctrine.

Web Pages Referenced

Akin, Jimmy. *"Did Jesus Say Adultery Is Grounds for Divorce?"* Catholic Answers Magazine, 7/1/2000, www.catholic.com/magazine/print-edition/did-jesus-say-adultery-is-grounds-for-divorce

Blessitt, Arthur, blessitt.com/miles-jesus-and-mary-walked, web page with estimates of how far Jesus walked in his lifetime.

Gilb, Lora. *"A Closer Look at 'Word for Word' Bible Translation"* Patterns of Evidence, 3/17/2023, www.patternsofevidence.com/2023/03/17/a-closer-look-at-word-for-word-bible-translation

Staples, Tim. *"Is Purgatory in the Bible?"* Catholic Answers Magazine, 2014, www.catholic.com/magazine/online-edition/is-purgatory-in-the-bible

Bible Gateway, www.biblegateway.com, Great site for comparing bible passages in different translations of the Bible.

Catholic Answers, www.catholic.com, is the world's largest database of answers about the beliefs and practices of the Catholic faith.

"Bible Translations Bestsellers, Best of 2022", Evangelical Christian Publishers Association ECPA https://christianbookexpo.com/bestseller/translations.php?id=BO22

"Genealogy of Christ" Catholic Encyclopedia. 1907-1912 www.catholic.com/encyclopedia/genealogy-of-christ

"Porneia Definition" Never Thirsty, Like The Master Ministries, www.neverthirsty.org/bible-qa/qa-archives/question/what-is-meaning-of-greek-word-porneia-in-bible/

"Porneia Definition" Strong's G4202 Greek Lexicon https://www.blueletterbible.org/lexicon/g4202/esv/tr/ss1/0-1/

About the Author

Douglas A. Leas was born and raised in Florida and attended a Methodist church in his youth. His religious journey has been circuitous. He has no particular religious credentials; he is not a minister and does not have degrees in theology. Rather, he is an educated man with a keen interest in understanding who Jesus was and what he taught, with the capability of doing research, summarizing it, and sharing the results with others.

He has earned BS and MS degrees in Computer Science and a Ph.D. in Educational Technology. He was a software engineer for thirty years, primarily in the telecommunications, aerospace, and internet industries. After that, he was a computer science professor for ten years.

If you would like to provide constructive feedback about this book or if you would like to ask questions, he will review all messages sent to JLT@GrizPress.com and may, at his discretion, address questions on the blog for this book at www.GrizPress.com/JesusTeachings. Please keep it civil; any messages that are not will be deleted.

Back cover images:

Upper Left: Alpha and Omega, the first and last letters in the Greek alphabet, are used to refer to Christ and God in the Book of Revelation.

Upper Right: The ichthys or fish symbol was used by early Christians to identify each other. One person would draw an arc and the other would fill in the other arc to make the fish. The letters ΙΧΘΥΣ are Greek for "fish" and are an acronym, each letter is the first letter of the following words: Ἰησοῦς Χρῑστός Θεοῦ Υἱός Σωτήρ which mean Jesus, Christ, God, Son, Savior.

Bottom Left: The Ichthys Wheel, a wheel-like symbol created by overlaying the letters ΙΧΘΥΣ from the ichthys on top of each other, used by early Christians to identify each other.

Bottom Center: A cross disguised as an anchor, one of the earliest Christian symbols found in many forms as far back as the first century. The symbol shown is modeled after one found in the Catacombs of Saint Domitilla in Rome.

Bottom Right: A symbol for Christ created by overlaying the first two letters, Chi and Rho, of the word Χρῑστός, which means Christ in Greek.

credit the book and the author.

Statutes vs. Status
presentation and delivery are
everything.

Full life bible (amazon)
(Study)

Sources   CSHB   N IV
                           Passion KJV
                           MSG   NLT
presentation next Monday
Ps. 63 - amos9 5 translations
Is. 40 =
~~Jeremiah 54:17~~

which one did you understand
two commentaries Matthew Henry
what is Holy Spirit saying.

Made in the USA
Middletown, DE
29 April 2024